Life after 60? Yes!

Life after 60? Yes!

✦

Choices for Managing the Third Part of Your Life

John Alva Morford, Ed.D.
Julie Yearsley Hungar, Ed.D.
Delight Carter Willing, Ed.D.

iUniverse, Inc.
New York Lincoln Shanghai

Life after 60? Yes!
Choices for Managing the Third Part of Your Life

iUniverse books may be ordered through booksellers or by contacting:

iUniverse
2021 Pine Lake Road, Suite 100
Lincoln, NE 68512
www.iuniverse.com
1-800-Authors (1-800-288-4677)

ISBN-13: 978-0-595-37538-7 (pbk)
ISBN-13: 978-0-595-81931-7 (ebk)
ISBN-10: 0-595-37538-3 (pbk)
ISBN-10: 0-595-81931-1 (ebk)

Printed in the United States of America

To
Our spouses and families
from whom
we learn new things every day

Contents

Information and advice on wills; on health, life and long-term care insurance; on caring for family members and preparing for death offer assistance for the decisions we all must make in these matters.

Many options for using your time are open to you in your 60s and beyond. Choices include spending time on family and friends, learning, volunteering, recreation, arts and travel.

We all need to feel our lives have meaning, and as we live the last third of our lives, there are many ways we can continue or expand our spiritual dimensions.

Here is a summary checklist to help you with the choices that will make the last third of your life long, healthy and meaningful.

1

Change and Choices: The Sixties Transition

When Terry Aronson was offered early retirement at age 62 from the bank he'd worked for since he left school, it knocked the wind out of his sails. "I thought my mid-life crisis was tough," he said, "but it was nothing compared to this one. Since I went to work full-time and got married, in my twenties, I haven't faced anything with this kind of impact on the rest of my life."

Like most of us, Terry had never thought about the kind of challenges people face in their sixties as holding both opportunity and danger. On the opportunity side, he could anticipate spending quality time with his wife, his three sons and their families, time he'd never had while working his way up in his organization. Both he and his wife, Karen, were in good health and enjoyed hiking together. He'd be able to perfect his fly-fishing technique, maybe get involved in local party politics, and finally build the cabinets for his basement workroom.

All that sounded great. But financially, Terry hadn't made it to the big-time. Now he had a good job as manager of a small branch of the bank; it supported a pleasant life and had enabled Karen to stay home while their boys were young. She had worked for the last 15 years in a craft store, but they hadn't been consistent in keeping to their savings plan. Something always seemed to come up—college for the boys, upkeep on a boat, surgery that kept Karen from working for several months.

They would have Social Security and a pension from the bank, though since it had been purchased by a large national bank, he was uncertain how his pension would be affected. In any case, that wouldn't be enough to maintain their current lifestyle. For that, Terry would need to get another job. At 62, with the economy in the doldrums, that might be a challenge, but with his background as an accountant, he was confident he could find something. Of course, if he did find a job, he'd be postponing the opportunity side of retirement for a few more years.

Does this sound familiar? Are you or someone you know facing choices of this magnitude? Here's the good news: We do have choices about the way we will live in the last third of our lives. A few things we can't control–getting older, dying, the economy. But the choices we can and do make will have a great deal to do with how well we live and how we handle getting older.

This message is especially pertinent for people who are approaching their sixties and for children whose parents are nearing retirement age. But really, it's never too early to begin making the choices that will prepare you to find pleasure and satisfaction–perhaps more than you've ever enjoyed–when you face the life changes of the sixties.

Make no mistake, as you move into your sixties and beyond, the changes will be major. Perhaps the most dramatic adult transitions of all are the ones most people make during this time. It's the time when, if you work outside your home, you might expect to retire from that career. Your parenting days are most likely behind you. You might be ready to move to another town, another climate, another country. Or you may choose, as Terry Aronson did, to stay put, take a part-time job, and begin easing into a more leisurely though less affluent style of living.

The choices open to Terry, and to most Americans today, were simply not available to the great majority of sixty-year-olds until the last half of the 20th Century. The introduction of Social Security and the spread of pension plans have made retirement affordable, and the great strides in health care and nutrition have given many of us the longevity to enjoy it. The result is an explosion of possibilities for a gratifying life after sixty. People now in their 60s, 70s and 80s are blazing the trail, but the real impact will come from the baby boomers as they reach their late 50s and early 60s. If you are a boomer looking ahead, you face the potential for many years of enjoyment and satisfaction–if you make the choices that are right for you.

Not everyone will be blessed with the good health and good pension plan that provide the strongest foundation for enjoying this time. The economic playing field is not level, and the bursting of the 90s dot.com bubble showed us that some kinds of bad luck are uninsurable. But even if you are not as well-off as you had hoped to be, even if your health limits your activity, you are likely to have more choices, more possibilities for making your life worthwhile, if you are prepared to look for them and take advantage of them.

The normal path of development throughout our adult lives includes fairly stable periods followed by periods of internal turmoil and transition. During these times, we take another look at who we are, how we relate to others, and what we want to do with our lives. These stages give us the chance to grow, but they carry the risk of decline as well. Our success or failure in dealing with these transitions determines how well we move on through the important phases of our lives.

For most of us, the two most important transitions are those from adolescence to adulthood, around age twenty, and from daily routine work to freedom, typically in our 60s. These two transitions are critical because they have lasting impact on the rest of our lives. As young adults, we make important choices about crucial issues—education, careers, spouses, places to live, and basic values systems. While we may move on to other choices, directions set in those early years continue to have an impact. The next time we are likely to face choices of such lasting impact is when we are in our sixties and have to decide what to do with the unprecedented free time that suddenly becomes ours to use, wisely or not.

We are constrained in the years between these two transition points by early commitments we have made. We must earn money. We must raise and educate our children. Our choice of where to live is limited by job and family, and so on. It's not until our 60s that most of us reach the point where paid work becomes optional and we are free of day-to-day child raising. Then we once again face choices as significant as those made in early adulthood. Suddenly, we can choose whether or not to keep working for pay, to stay in our home or move, go back to school or perfect our golf game–or both.

What has made this newfound freedom possible? Two factors stand out–better health, leading to increased life expectancy, and the general prosperity and improved pensions that enable people to stop working while they are still in good shape. The fastest growing groups in our population are those over 65 and over 85. As recently as the early years of the twentieth century people on average died within three years of retirement. Now 15 years is normal and 25 or more is not unusual—and this increased life expectation shows every sign of expanding further.

Not only are we living longer but we are much healthier than earlier generations. Not long ago people in their 60s were considered "old" or "young old." Now sixty-year-olds are more commonly described as in "late middle age." And the number and proportion of mentally and physically able seventy-and eighty-year-olds increases every day, vastly expanding the impact of the life choices they made during their sixties.

Only since the middle of the twentieth century have economic resources been available to allow vast numbers of citizens to live decently without continuing to work for pay. Even today in developing parts of the world, those who do live into their sixties and beyond continue to work until they can no longer do so, the way all people were expected to do only a few generations ago. But for the average American today, the opportunity to retire offers choices denied to all but the richest and healthiest in past centuries.

How, then, do we prepare for making wise choices during this important transitional stage of life? Each transition holds both opportunity for growth and risk of decline. The way we deal with our successive life transitions defines us. In a very real way, we are the choices we've made in earlier transitions. Knowing what the key issues are for a given transition and forging an approach that works for you can make all the difference. That's what this book is about: it's a guide to help you prepare for and navigate successfully through this transition to the third part of your life.

In each of the chapters that follow we cover a major area of choice for living well during your sixties and after. We report on what the experts have to say and we give you real-life examples that show how to navigate the changes and make the choices well–or the consequences of not doing them well. Then we conclude with a descriptive list of resources that will give you further information to help you make the best choices for you and your family. Chapter 2 examines relationships, which have been proven to be central to healthy aging. In Chapter 3 one of the most important choices for most sixty-year-olds is discussed–whether to retire or to continue working. The next two chapters consider physical and mental health, both of which are keys to aging well. Financial issues are reviewed in Chapter 6, and other personal matters, such as wills and insurance, are discussed in Chapter 7. Options for the use of the free time that most of us can look forward to in our sixties are discussed in Chapter 8. We deal in Chapter 9 with the search for meaning, including spiritual and religious issues facing those in their 60s and beyond. Finally, in Chapter 10 we summarize and provide a checklist of the thirty most important choices you face during your sixties.

Your sixties offer the promise of unprecedented choices for the third stage of your life. We hope this guide will play a part in making it a great time.

THE AUTHORS

As we began this book, Julie had recently completed her sixties, Delight was about to begin hers, and John was nearing the end of his sixties decade. Our varied life experiences before and during our sixties pervade everything we've written, so we want to share something about ourselves with you.

John. From 1963 until my retirement in 1995 I was a professor and administrator in two Jesuit universities, John Carroll University in Ohio and Seattle University. Throughout my years in Ohio I also taught developmental psychology and came to realize that the accepted authorities incorrectly assumed that development ended in early adulthood. That realization led many years later to this book.

From 1973 through 1995, I served at Seattle University, first as Dean of the School of Education, then as founding chair of the Doctoral Program in Educational Leadership. During my final years at Seattle University, Adult Psychology and Learning became my favorite course. I realized though that there still was little available on the opportunities and challenges people face during their 60s. This book evolved from that realization.

Since "retiring" in 1995, I have spent time with the Jesuits in Nepal, managed the food bank and the dinner for the homeless at my church, served as treasurer and board member for Washington/ Chile Partners of the Americas, and served as a consultant to inner-city Catholic schools. I also spent the summer of 2001 in radiation treatment for prostate cancer, which now seems to be in remission.

Julie. After going back to college to become more employable when my children were all in school, I was fortunate to land a teaching job at Seattle Central Community College. As a "returning woman" myself, I was especially gratified to see many other women–divorced, widowed, or just wanting to learn–blossom in my classes. Seattle Central was, and is, a laboratory for understanding people of all ages and every other kind of diversity as they seek to improve their lives through education.

Ten years later I went back to school once more, this time for a doctorate in education, with John as my dissertation advisor. That led to administrative jobs with the Seattle Community Colleges until I retired in 1995. Since retiring, I have completed two books on education with Dr. Janet Lieberman and written a number of articles and book chapters. Through service on several volunteer boards I have gained insight into the lives of the homeless, the aging, and children of the urban ghetto.

Delight. I married between my junior and senior years of college, got my teaching credential and taught junior high school English. As my marriage ended, I returned to Seattle to adjust to life alone in my 30s. I was fortunate to "luck into" a job at Renton Technical College establishing an Adult Basic Education and English as a Second Language program. I served in a variety of administrative roles there over the next sixteen years.

Being drawn to Adult Education, I earned a Master's degree in Adult Education at Seattle University and then a doctorate in the university's innovative program in educational leadership. In 1987 I joined the faculty of this program, and later developed a new Master's Degree in Adult Education and Training. I worked in that program until my retirement in December 2003.

I was married for thirty-two years to Shippen Willing, who was significantly older than I, so I moved through his sixties, his seventies, and then his eighties with him. I have observed how he stayed active physically and mentally by making many of the life-style choices we recommend in this book. His death in April 2005, like his life, was quiet and peaceful.

In the past several years, I have had both my hips replaced and have been treated for breast cancer, which is currently in remission. These experiences have made me especially aware of the aging process and the need to live a successful and fulfilling last third of my life. From these experiences comes my interest in the topics of this book.

A NOTE ON REFERENCES AND RESOURCES

Below is a list of the source books referred to in more than one of the following chapters. They will not usually be re-listed in the resources of later chapters. In the chapters that follow resources will usually include several general books on the chapter topic, organizations relevant to the topics discussed in the chapter, web sites related to the general topic of the chapter or to major sub-topics, and other works deserving special mention. Given the scope of the topics, no attempt will be made to provide comprehensive resources. Rather, we will include items that will allow the reader easily to find further works on topics of special interest.

Each of the books listed below will be referred to frequently in the chapters that follow. Every one of them is worth reading if you want to know more about later adulthood.

Perls, T. & Silver, M. (1999). *Living to 100: Lessons in Living to Your Maximum Potential at Any Age.* New York: Basic Books.

Seligman, M. (2002). *Authentic Happiness: Using the New Positive Psychology to Realize Your Potential for Lasting Fulfillment.* New York: Free Press.

Seligman, M. (1990). *Learned Optimism: How to Change Your Mind and Your Life.* New York: Pocket Books.

Sheehy, G. (1995). *New Passages: Mapping Your Life across Time.* New York: Random House.

Snowdon, D. (2001). *Aging with Grace: What the Nun Study Teaches Us about Leading Longer, Healthier and More Meaningful Lives.* New York: Bantam Books.

Stevens-Long, J. & Commons, M. (1992). *Adult Life (4ᵗʰ edition).* Mountain View, CA: Mayfield Publishing Company.

Vaillant, G. (2002). *Aging Well: Surprising Guideposts to a Happier Life from the Landmark Harvard Study of Adult Development.* Boston: Little, Brown & Co.

2

Relationships: The Key to Happy Aging

Joe and Judy truly enjoy their Thursday mornings together. Joe, a retired federal employee in his early 60s, and Judy, a retired English teacher nearing 70, spend four or five hours each Thursday driving all over the city picking up food supplies for their local food bank—and discussing everything from the economy in Latin America to the evolution of Alzheimer's disease, with a few sports scores and opera critiques thrown in.

They have a lot of conversation to catch up on today because Joe and his wife have been away for a couple weeks visiting his ailing mother, age 92, and attending a class reunion. Nonetheless, today both are in a bit of a rush because Joe needs to arrive early for the end-of-the-year ceremony at the inner-city school where his daughter teaches and he tutors. And Judy is meeting her teenage grandson to help him plan his Eagle Scout project, which is to build a roof over the outside storage area at the local food bank for which Judy volunteers. Following that, she and her husband are due at dinner with a group of her former students who meet on a regular basis.

This real life example illustrates the type of choices about relationships that research has proven to be most likely to lead to a happy, healthy life among those 60 and above. Humans are social animals so it is not surprising that isolation often leads to both physical and mental decay. While there are great variations in the amount and type of interpersonal relationships needed by and available to individuals, the drives to love and be loved, to hear and be heard, to receive and to share are common to all. In fact, according to a recent article by Katherine Griffin, "Friends: the Secret to a Longer Life," over 100 studies have shown that by choosing to develop and maintain good relationships you can boost your "chances of surviving life-threatening illnesses," upgrade your immune system, improve your mental health, and live longer. Other studies have shown that good relationships also improve your self-esteem, help you overcome or compensate for disabilities, and make your life more meaningful.

Of course, for those 60 and above relationships come in many sizes and shapes—spouses, children, parents, grandchildren, siblings, other extended family members, friends, work or volunteer peers, fellow association members, and even pets. Within these, a variety of types of relationships exist, ranging from friendly but not personal to intimate and even sexual. In this chapter we will look at what research says about these questions:

- How important are marital relationships?

- Are sexual relationships still important to those over sixty?

- Do relationships with extended family, friends, peers, and pets also make a difference?

- And, because all relationships have not only beginnings but also endings, how can those in their sixties best deal with loss and death?

Oliver and his niece Andrea lived lives that on the surface seemed quite similar. Yet, because of how they developed their relationships the reality proved much different.

Oliver never needed a lot of friends. In fact, from his 40s on, he and his wife Denita lived in remote northwestern Montana on a farm with no electricity or running water. "We've got each other, a lantern, a pump and a path," he used to say, "What more do we need?" While Denita made friends with neighbors, Oliver never felt the need. Rare visits from one of his sisters or from a nephew were about the only contact he had with the outside world other than to sell his farm products.

During their mid-sixties Denita fell ill and died. Once family members who had come to her funeral left, Oliver made no attempt to contact anyone. For a year or so he went through his daily routine on the farm. Then one night he stuck his shotgun in his mouth and ended his loneliness. It took some time for his body to be found. There was no funeral.

Like Oliver, Andrea spent much of her adult life on a farm. The first person in her family to complete college, she married Larry, a young farmer near Walla Walla, and settled in as a farm wife and mother. However, in contrast with Oliver, she also became active in area church, intellectual, and social affairs.

Again like Oliver, in her sixties she lost her spouse when Larry, a heavy smoker who also distributed farm chemicals, succumbed to lung cancer. At this, Andrea chose to leave the farm and move to Walla Walla to be nearer friends, church and social activities. From then until a short time before she died of natural causes at 90, Andrea remained active helping the less fortunate, joining in book club discussions, and communicating with family and friends on a regular basis. Through genealogical study, she even proved she had an ancestor who fought in the Revolutionary War so she could join the local Daughters of the American Revolution chapter.

Following her death surrounded by family and friends, people of all ages and social status attended her memorial to honor the memory of their friend.

How important are marital relationships? "Marriage is not only important to healthy aging, it is often the cornerstone of adult resilience," according to the findings of what is probably the most important longitudinal study ever done on adult development and aging, the Harvard Study of Adult Development. In fact, that study, *Aging Well: Surprising Guideposts to a Happier Life from the Landmark Harvard Study of Adult Development* by George Vaillant, M.D., showed that a stable marriage in late middle age predicted both good physical and mental health in the 70s and 80s. On the other hand, a bad marriage caused "negative aging at age 70" just as it had earlier at midlife. Similarly, as reported in *New Passages: Mapping Your Life Across Time,* when Gail Sheehy, author of several of the most popular books on adult development, followed male business graduates as they aged, she found, "The comfort of mature love is the single most important determinant of older men's outlook on life. *Ninety* percent of the happiest HBS men are in love with their wives today and say they have grown closer since the children left…. Of the whole group studied, 88 percent are still married to Wife Number One."

The good news is that for those who remain married into their 60s and beyond, research reported by Judith Stevens-Long and Michael Commons in *Adult Life,* one of the great texts on adult development, shows that by age 60 marital satisfaction for most has rebounded to near the level of newlyweds and that by age 70 it typically has risen to a plateau at its highest level ever. As Vaillant puts it in *Aging Well*, "One of the more exciting Study findings was that after 70 the marriages of generative Study members got still better."

So, why worry? Because none of this happens automatically. You have to choose to spend the time, energy and commitment needed to make it happen. To paraphrase Dr. Vaillant's comment on marriage: Marriage is hard work, requiring "a healthy dose of tolerance, commitment, maturity, and a sense of humor." When discussing the research findings on mature love, Stevens-Long and Commons describe the tasks involved: "The problem occurs because maturity and mature love are usually conceptualized as an achievement, or a state, rather than an ongoing process or struggle. If development occurs in adult life, then the self and the loved one are always changing..... Change implies the need to reevaluate and reintegrate one's view of both the self and the other. Integration is not something one achieves; it is something one struggles to maintain."

One of the key choices involved in the struggle to maintain a good marriage involves what researchers call "individuation and fusion." Developing and maintaining a proper balance between individuation and fusion often becomes critical when people retire and begin spending larger amounts of time together. This means you have to discover how to meet your spouse's needs and accept her or his identity without diminishing yourself or dominating your spouse. Failing to fuse can lead you to isolation; whereas failing to individuate can make it impossible for you to be self-sufficient. Simply put, during their 60s married couples must choose to be both close and separate, intimate and liberated, one and two.

You would have to say the marriage of Adam and Theresa is exemplary in this regard. They've raised four sons and have maintained close ties with both their immediate and their extended families, who recently helped them celebrate their 50th anniversary. They share a number of activities, but each of them is involved in interests that are not mutual. Theresa is an avid hiker—she hikes in the Pacific Northwest, in the Southwest, and in Europe with friends or hiking groups; Adam likes deep-sea fishing and golf, which he enjoys with his group of like-minded friends. Whatever sacrifices the couple has made to accommodate their commitment to divergent interests appear to have strengthened their marriage.

Choosing to maintain and even improve your marriage during your 60s pays great dividends. However, the bad news is that for many, especially women, the choice does not exist. Only about 40 percent of women over 65 are married compared to 80 percent of men. And when marriage ends through death or divorce for those over 60, few women remarry but most men do. For those facing their 70s and beyond without a spouse, choosing to develop alternate intimate relationships becomes even more important, as we will discuss shortly. But, first, let us look at what research says about sexual relationships for those 60 and beyond.

Are sexual relationships still important to those over sixty?
For women and most men 60 and above, the sexual drive no longer relates to reproducing the species. Nonetheless, the desire for and value of intimate relationships usually remains strong. The research on this can be summarized as follows: For as long as they live most people desire and are capable of sexual relations. However desirable and useful a positive sexual relationship is to aging adults, if neces-

sary, most older people are capable of living happy, healthy lives without it. There will be great variations from person to person and couple to couple as to the desirable frequency of intimate relationships as well as to the nature of sexual relationships. As is true at younger ages, sexual intimacy offers both great rewards and great dangers for those over 60. Wise choices regarding sexuality and sexual relationships can promote health, happiness and long life; bad choices can bring despair, illness and even death. Let us look at what studies have shown us about sex in the last third of life.

In *Adult Life* Stevens-Long and Commons report on a range of findings concerning sexuality in late middle age and beyond. First, they point out: "The best predictor of sexual activity in later life is previous sexual activity. Most sexually active people report only a modest decline in frequency of sexual activity from age fifty-five on into their seventies." They add, "Although Masters and Johnson (1966) may have overstated the case…when they summed it up, 'Use it or lose it,' their advice remains basically sound." Then Stevens-Long and Commons report on several somewhat contradictory findings on sexual activity involving those over 60.

On the one hand, they report that the Duke Longitudinal Studies of Normal Aging "found that sexual activity predicted health, happiness, and longevity among all the participants [male and female]." Surely this finding is related to those on marriage discussed above. The happier married state reported by those over 60 logically should lead to improved sexual relationships. In a virtuous circle, this should lead to even greater happiness with the marriage, resulting in gains in mental and physical health as will be discussed in later chapters. On the other hand, Stevens-Long and Commons also report that "although there is an association between sexual activity and life satisfaction,…sex is not essential to happiness, nor is it pre-requisite to mental health." In other words, even though aging people may continue to desire sexual relationships, when they are not available for one reason or another, most can accept the loss and get on with life.

In *Living to 100* Perls and Silver discuss the most common reasons older adults cease sexual relations or suffer from sexual dysfunction. As might be expected, by far "the most common and important reason for cessation of sex among older people is the lack of a partner; this is particularly a problem among older women, many of whom are widowed." Sexual dysfunction, however, most commonly arises from illness or as a side effect of medication or other treatment. At times, medical personnel may ignore possible sexual dysfunction side effects because a patient is elderly, so it's important that you remain alert to this factor. Often less damaging treatments or medications are available. Or devices and corrective medications such as hormones or Viagra exist to compensate for loss of sexual function. It's perfectly clear that in this regard "old dogs can learn new tricks" and enjoy improved relationships in the process.

John's experience with radiation treatment for his prostate cancer involved several choices each of which had the potential for negative sexual side-effects. All current treatments for prostate cancer include the possibility of sudden or gradual impotence. John chose external beam radiation, in part, because it was less likely to result in sudden impotence. However, as often happens with external radiation treatment, he has suffered gradual, partial impotence. Until the recent development of Viagra and its peers that would have been a permanent disability. Fortunately, that is no longer the case. Caution: taking any medication can have bad side effects. For example testosterone which current ads claim enhances sexual prowess has been shown to promote the growth of prostate cancer.

Research questioning the safety of the most common hormone replacement therapy (HRT) has created a dilemma for some older women whose sex life has been enhanced by the effects of these drugs. For ten years, Julie had taken the hormone medication recommended by her doctors. During that time she enjoyed gratifying sexual relations with her husband, something she hadn't really expected to experience during her sixties. Following the widely reported research pointing to health risks of HRT, she stopped taking her medication and over time found she had less interest and less pleasure in sex. She consulted a naturopathic physician, who recommended a more natural form of hormone therapy. Although it has not yet been proven, this medication is thought to be safer than the more common form. For a while Julie used the new therapy while being aware that it was still a gamble. Since then further reports have led her to abandon the therapy entirely.

Finally, as you make your choices during your 60s about sexual relationships, remember two rules that apply at any age: Sexual relationships involve the very essence of human life and love. Therefore, even when pregnancy is no longer an issue, commitment and love remain essential. Aging hearts break as easily as young ones. Second, being 60 and above in no way provides immunity from sexually transmitted diseases—including AIDs. A recent upsurge in HIV infection among elderly women illustrates how dangerous promiscuous or unprotected sex can be at any age.

Heather, whose husband had died some years earlier, joined a square dance group with the hope of finding romance in her sixties. She was overjoyed when seventy-two year-old Luke, the most sought after man in the group, ask her for a date. Over several months she again enjoyed sharing her life with a male friend. Unfortunately, until it was too late she never realized they were sharing the AIDs virus.

Choosing sexual partners and activities wisely remains an important part of all life transitions—including in your 60s. Should you need help in these matters, several of the works in the chapter resources discuss sexual issues in depth. Beyond that, reputable sex therapists, who can be found in any city these days, are available to assist you.

For those who lack a marriage and/or sex partner, developing and maintaining other positive relationships becomes doubly important. Therefore, we will now examine what studies tell us about other relationships such as those within extended families, between friends, and in settings involving work, volunteering, or social activities. Relationships with pets will also be touched upon.

Do relationships with extended family, friends, peers, and pets also make a difference? *At 60 Priscilla, a poet and teacher who did us the honor of critiquing our manuscript, savors living alone, having ended her 20-year marriage 12 years ago. In her essay "Turning Sixty" she says, "I live alone, happily. Every day I savor the pleasures and privileges of living by myself. These range from the green silence at dusk (replacing bickering over dinner arrangements) to the pleasures of arranging rooms in such a way that they shelter the soul and nurture the creative work." However, Priscilla has continuing complex relationships with a great variety of people through her teaching, her work with writing groups, her many friends, her poetry readings, and not least through serving as webmaster for a prominent web site (www.historylink.org/).*

Her life is a beautiful illustration of how you can live alone without being isolated or lonely.

Commonly, however, in their 60s people retire and lose the complex relationships developed through decades of work. Thus, as Vaillant points out, it is essential that you "replace work mates with another social network." However, the composition of that "social network" can vary greatly depending on your personality and other factors in your life, such as where you live.

As is pointed out in *Adult Life*, "There is good reason to believe that older people are more different from one another than are the young." For some, especially introverted men, an intimate relationship with a spouse may be the only really close friendship desired or needed. For most, however, a greater variety of friendships is essential to a happy, fulfilling life. Yet even then the range remains great. You may find close relationships with your children and grandchildren sufficient where another person may feel the need to develop friendships with a dozen or more people in various settings. Only you can decide what your needs are. As one author put it, "It may be that...if you think you have enough friends, you will be happy."

The research consistently shows that older women typically deal with developing needed friendships more easily than do men, so if you are a man in your 60s, you may need to make a more conscious decision to develop and maintain close relationships. For men and women alike, the absolutely critical thing is to make whatever effort is necessary to avoid becoming isolated and lonely.

The need for a variety of positive relationships may be the single most important finding of the Harvard Study of Adult Development as reported in *Aging Well*. When discussing how to grow old with grace, the first and the last of the six characteristics Vaillant lists involve relationships. The first emphasizes caring about others, maintaining social utility and helping others. And the last involves both attempting to "maintain contact and intimacy with old friends" and remembering that "the seeds of love must be eternally resown"—a favorite quote of his from Ann Morrow Lindbergh. Elsewhere, when he summarizes the five "lessons for successful aging," three of the lessons involve relationships: "Remember, life is a journey and always resow the seeds of love." "Service to others makes life interesting and surrounds one with love in return." "Biology flows downhill, so choose loving parents and help and learn from your own children [and grandchildren]."

On this last point Vaillant emphasizes over and over the importance of both giving to and taking from the younger generation—whether that involves your own progeny or other younger persons. "Paradoxically," he says, "the Study members who learned the most from the next generation had been also the most successful at caring for them. Successful aging requires continuing to learn new things and continuing to take people in." He summarizes this wonderfully: "Thus, when we are old, our lives become the sum of all whom we have loved."

Julie's career as Vice-Chancellor of the Seattle Community College system kept her too busy to give much time to family until she retired, but then she concentrated on grandparenting. Six-year-old Dylan made her day with his serious announcement while the two of them were drinking "tea" at the playroom table. He said, "You know, Grandma, I'm really glad you got this house, because we've had a lot of good times here." She treasures that memory, especially now that Dylan is in his teens; she knows their bond is strong enough to withstand the rigors of teenagerdom.

For most of us, families are at the center of such relationships. When discussing how important resilience is to good health, Vaillant points out that "part of resilience is the ability to find the loving and health-giving individuals within one's social matrix wherever they may be. This is why extended families are one of the great boons to mental health." And two things typically happen during the 60s transition to facilitate developing closer relationships with family members: First, as Sheehy found in her study, by the mid-sixties there seems to be a natural tendency to focus more on family and friends and less on career. And, second, for most of us the time becomes available to develop continuing friendships and reignite dormant ones. Visiting long-lost siblings or cousins is not unusual among those in their 60s. In fact, studies reported in *Adult Life* indicate that for those above 60, four-fifths "feel close to at least one sibling." Also several studies have found that the ability to forget and forgive old grievances "leads to successful aging more often than does nursing old resentments."

Shortly after retiring from twenty years as an accountant, Terry Szmagala remembered how much she and her cousin Hank had enjoyed being together when they were young. Somehow, with jobs, family, and the fact that their spouses disliked one another, they had drifted apart years ago. Having heard that Hank, now widowed, had recently retired too, Terry invited him out to lunch to talk about old times and get reacquainted. As she put it, "Odd as it may seem, we took off just as if we had never been apart. We talked a lot, laughed a lot and cried a little that day. And ever since we never let a week pass without talking—at least by phone. After all those years, he is once again one of my best friends."

The changing nature of extended families will surely affect the choices boomers make about relationships during their 60s transition. Data reported in *Adult Life* indicate that "fifty percent of people over sixty-five are members of four generation families and 20 percent of females over eighty are part of five generation families." Extended families no longer look like pyramids with a mass of youngsters and few oldsters. Rather, "the American family becomes a long-lived 'bean-pole' with more living generations, each of which has fewer members." In the years ahead it will be commonplace for those in their 60s to have living parents as well as children and grandchildren—and even great grandchildren. Thus, sixty-year-olds with responsibility both for aged parents and grandchildren will become increasingly common.

"I loved it when our triplet grandchildren were born, and it has been great to have my mom live so long in good health." Janice explains, adding, "I must admit, however, that at times it's been about all I can deal with. It sure hasn't been what I thought retirement would be like."

Shortly before Janice and her husband Bob decided to retire, one of their daughters, a career professional, surprised them by giving birth to triplets. Concerned about her daughter's health, Janice agreed to retire and become a part-time care giver for her new grandchildren. Unfortunately, very soon thereafter Janice's mother, who was in her early 90s and had always been in good health, began to need help too.

Janice shared assisting her mother, who lived an hour away, with her sister who lived near their mom. For some time she both assisted her daughter several days a week and commuted other days to help her mother. Her love and devotion to her family sustained her, but friends noticed gradual effects from the stress involved.

Fortunately, after a year or so of this schedule, her daughter's situation improved so helping with the triplets required less time. Also, Bob decided to retire too, which freed them to move much closer to Janice's mother. Now they are able to get away at times and do some of the things they had planned for after retirement. When asked how she could handle it all, Janice downplays her effort, saying, "You just have to keep your priorities straight. My children, my grandchildren and my mom mean everything to me. Despite the strain at times, it is a privilege to be needed and able to help."

Happily, the research makes clear that in most instances two-way giving and receiving up and down the beanpole are the norm, not the exception. In fact, research shows that "people of all ages are much more willing to give than to receive." So, being open to receiving help and love from family and friends may be one of the skills a sixty-year-old should choose to hone. In fact, when Vaillant lists items found to be important to healthy aging, he concludes by saying, "Use the telephone...ask for help."

Ruth can attest to the value of this advice, but it wasn't easy for her to follow. She is a highly capable woman who carved out a professional career in public relations after she was widowed. She planned well for her retirement so that she would not need to depend on either of her two sons in her old age. When she realized how genuinely depressed she was after a series of minor but recurring health problems, she finally and hesitantly called one of her sons. She learned that he and his brother had felt rebuffed by her constant declarations of independence and were eager to involve her in their family lives.

Another finding reported in *Adult Life* adds an important caveat to this good news: "Elderly people who had no contact with anyone except their children exhibited negative morale." Clearly, for most people the greatest benefits come from having positive relationships both within the family and with others outside.

One of the most interesting findings from the study of people who live to be 100 illustrates this. As would be expected, Perls and Silver found "nearly all centenarians have many meaningful relationships. They are almost never 'loners.'…Few centenarians would pass for matinee idols, but they seem to have one thing in common: They attract people." In the face of this and other studies showing the importance of married companionship, Perls and Silver were surprised to find that 14 percent of the women centenarians had never married. However, it turned out that these women had wisely developed and replaced relationships as they aged, so that even at over 100 "these lifelong single women were surrounded by loving people of all ages." Interestingly, every male centenarian in the study had been married, most for a very long time. This, and the fact that relatively few men survive to 100, led Perls and Silver to say, "Men, however, seemed even more dependent on relationships than women."

While spouses, lifelong friends, and extended families may satisfy relationship needs for some seniors, most will benefit from expanded relationships. For one thing, commitments and benefits vary among types of relationships. For example, friendship with a casual golfing buddy can provide a relaxed give and take that may be hard to maintain with an ill parent or struggling child. And, as Stevens-Long and Commons put it, "A strong social network may help people maintain positive self-regard and optimism, even in the most dire of circumstances. However unrealistic, positive self-regard correlates with happiness, contentment, the ability to care for others and the capacity for creative work." They add, "As long as you and your friends agree that you are doing OK, perhaps you are, regardless of how the situation looks to others." Finally, expanded relationships can provide greater opportunities for giving service, which has been shown to benefit the giver as well as the recipients.

The experience of Maria illustrates this point. Maria was widowed after ten years of marriage, and, having had no children, went back to work as an accountant. She engaged in a long relationship with a man who did not want a permanent partner and so she eventually broke this off. To fill the void in her life, she became a mainstay in the volunteer corps of a homeless shelter. The agency came to count on her organizing ability as well as her sunny personality, and she has gained a group of close friends among the staff and the gratitude of countless clients.

Commenting on the differences between aging business graduates who were high in well-being and those that were low, Sheehy confirms this idea: "Perhaps one of the reasons the highs have fewer aches and pains is that they concern themselves with others....The lows, in contrast, are very involved with themselves." She summarizes this by saying, "Thus, it is not dollars or titles that are most important to people in their sixties; it is the quality of meaningful human attachments and having something to be excited about."

In a later chapter we will describe in more detail the vast opportunities to use your new free time to expand your relationships through a variety of channels ranging from church groups to political involvement to charitable endeavors to artistic outlets to group travel to other learning activities and many more. Again, what will fit your needs, your time, and your inclinations may vary greatly from what your neighbor chooses to do. The important thing is to make your life more meaningful by getting involved, for as Snowdon put it in reporting on the Nun Study, "It has now been convincingly documented that marriage, membership in churches, clubs, or other social groups, and regular contact with family and friends all reduce the risk of death from the major killers, coronary disease and stroke."

Interestingly, at least some of the benefits from good relationships can come from having a friendly relationship with a pet. Many studies have shown that having an animal friend that adores you and lets you adore it in return can pay dividends in health and happiness, especially for those whose disabilities or life circumstances tend to isolate them. Stevens-Long and Commons report that when a group of older adults were consulted about the design of facilities for themselves, "Most insisted on being allowed to keep a pet—one woman commented that her cat was 'the only warm thing that has touched me in years.'" In general, however, pets should supplement, not replace, human relationships.

Before deciding to add a pet to your life during your 60s transition, you will want to consider several factors. Do you plan to travel a lot under circumstances where your pet could not accompany you? If so, unless you have pet support built into your other relationships, getting a pet may not be a good idea. Also, some pets require much more attention or more expenditures than others. Will you have the time and money to keep your pet healthy and happy? Remember pets range from tiny, inexpensive, short-lived and self-sustaining insects to expensive, long-lived, demanding dogs. What may work for your neighbor may not be best for you. Again, you need to analyze your own needs and situation carefully before deciding to add a pet to your life. Because many animals have relatively short life spans, dealing with the loss of a beloved pet often presents a challenge similar to that faced when a human relationship ends.

And, because all relationships have not only beginnings but also endings, how can those in their sixties best deal with loss and death? Dealing with loss and death is one of the constants in the last third of life. Loss can come in many forms to those over 60. It can come as retirement, widowhood, children leaving home, illness, divorce, physical or mental impairments, financial decline, leaving your own home, loss of personal independence, or the death of family members, friends or pets. How you deal with loss can make a huge difference in both your happiness and health.

Lauren's 80th birthday party celebrated a wonderful life. Children, grandchildren, great grandchildren, relatives and many friends honored her with remembrances of her love, kindness, generosity and perseverance in spite of losses during her 60s that might have crushed another person.

In her early 60s Lauren's life had seemed idyllic. She and her recently retired husband, Jerome, had planned carefully for their retirement and had moved permanently to the lake house they had been building for many years. Their three successful children and several young grandchildren, including two Cambodian orphans recently adopted by their daughter Sarah, brightened their lives. Then the losses began.

First, Jerome, a lifelong smoker, was found to have lung cancer. Despite receiving the best treatment available, within eighteen months he was gone. Suddenly, she had to live without "the nicest guy you'll ever meet," as family and friends often referred to Jerome. Before she could fully recover from that loss, another family tragedy called for her attention.

Her beautiful daughter's husband suddenly announced that he had found a new woman in another state and was leaving her and their adopted pre-school aged children. To help her daughter through that difficult time and to care for the children while her daughter worked, Lauren moved back from her beloved lake house to the city she had chosen to leave several years before. Sadly, the worst was yet to come.

As so often happens after such losses, within a year Sarah fell ill. At first it seemed a simple case of emotional and physical exhaustion, but when she did not respond to treatment, further exams showed she had cancer. As had been the case with her father, Sarah responded briefly to treatment only to learn that the cancer was terminal. In her late 60s, without her husband to support her, Lauren suddenly found herself the primary caregiver for a young granddaughter and grandson who in their short lives had been orphaned in Cambodia, adopted and moved to the US, abandoned by their adopted father, and then had watched their adopted mother die after a long illness.

As attested to by all who came to her 80th birthday celebration, Lauren not only survived those losses, she nourished others and helped them grow despite the pain they endured. Always a positive, hard working, competent woman with many friends, she met the challenge of loss and grew under it. Now in her early 80s she splits her time between the city and the lake place where she frequently entertains friends and her large extended family that now includes several great grandchildren.

The research on this topic is encouraging. The Duke Longitudinal Studies of Normal Aging found older people "exhibited the capacity to adapt to retirement, widowhood, children leaving home and even serious illness. None of these events appeared to produce long-term negative events." Similarly, Stevens-Long and Commons report that "older people are generally able to adapt to the loss of a spouse. Widowhood in later life is not accompanied by long-term negative effects on adjustment and, in fact, may signal an increase in life satisfaction if the dying spouse was extremely ill." This is not to say, however, that dealing with great loss is easy or painless.

Stevens-Long and Commons reflect on the effects of widowhood: "Acute grief occurs within a few days of bereavement and is severe for several months. Recovery usually takes place in twelve to eighteen months." They also point out that the quality of the recovery is best where resources such as education, money and friendships are the greatest. The depth of grief, however, will be most closely "related to the centrality of the spouse in the individual's married life." The more central, the deeper the grief.

Several other factors also affect how easily and completely you are likely to recover from serious loss. The nature of the loss matters. For example, the murder or suicide of a child or grandchild has been shown to be perhaps the most devastating type of loss. Often special support and therapy are needed to aid recovery in such cases. On the other hand, as we will see, most people recover rather quickly from the losses connected to retirement. That is true of launching children as well. Also, your own level of resilience or health at the time of a loss can affect your recovery. If you already lean toward depression and suffer a significant loss, you would be wise to seek help, which can range from support groups to professional therapy. See the resources for suggestions in this area.

A cautionary example is Elizabeth's situation. She continued to take care of her husband long after his Alzheimer's disease made it extremely difficult. Her own health suffered as a result, but she did not take time to attend to her own medical needs, despite the urging of friends. Shortly after she finally placed him in a nursing home, her husband died. Elizabeth had postponed needed knee surgery while caring for her husband. When, soon after his death, she went in for a checkup in preparation for the knee surgery, doctors found cancer as well. Fortunately, the tumor was safely removed, chemotherapy was effective, and she was then able to have her knee taken care of.

Research has shown that loss often has physiological effects that you must be prepared to deal with. For example, Stevens-Long and Commons say, "Studies have demonstrated that the levels of a very powerful group of hormones known as the corticosteroids increase during bereavement and remain high for a very long time. The death rates for bereaved people are much higher than those of the general population, and rates for infection and malignancy have been reported at 2.5 to 5 times the national average." In other words, at times of loss you must pay special attention to things that promote good health such as your diet, exercise, meaningful activities, and especially to your other relationships.

Vaillant's constant reminder to "resow the seeds of love" to maintain the relationships we have and also to replace those we have lost is most relevant here. Healthy aging clearly calls for being able to grieve loss, then put it behind us and get on with life. As the study of centenarians found, those who survive well into extreme old age all have lived through many great losses but "they are able to maintain their emotional focus and concentrate on survival."

A related challenge during your 60s transition comes from facing the ever increasing likelihood of your own death. As Sheehy puts it, "People you know are already dying. Their vacancy is a silent reminder that death could always crash the party any time. And with that changed perspective on death, there is a sense of time passing faster."

Interestingly, however, research reported in *Adult Life* shows "older people are not as anxious about death and dying as are the young." The researchers also indicate "that there are gender differences in death...with women expressing more anxiety than men." For those in their 60s the best approach may call for being prepared for death when it comes but concentrating on doing those things that make life worthwhile.

In later chapters we will discuss several issues related to being prepared for death, e.g., estate planning, wills, long-term care, directions for terminal health care and interment, and spiritual and religious factors. All of these have ramifications for your relationships and call for communicating about them with those affected. None of this, however, should be allowed to stand in the way of your choosing to continue to grow in your relationships and the other aspects of your life.

RESOURCES

Many of the book and web site resources listed in later chapters have relevance here—particularly those in the chapter on mental health. Here we list a few general books and web sites and then selected books and web sites for the specific topics covered in the chapter.

General Books:

Karren, K. (ed.). (2001). *Mind/Body Health: the Effects of Attitudes, Emotions, and Relationships (2nd edition)*. San Francisco: Benjamin/Cummings. This book contains long sections on various types of relationships as part of its presentation of research findings on how the mind affects health.

Keirsey, D. & Bates, M. (1984). *Please Understand Me (5th edition)*. Del Mar, CA: Prometheus Nemesis Books. This classic discussion of personality and temperament types as they relate to personal relationships has improved many lives including some of ours. It is also available in several other languages including Spanish.

Patterson, K., et al. (2002). *Crucial Conversations: Tools for Talking When Stakes Are High.* N.Y.: McGraw-Hill. This easy, inexpensive book can help all of us with one of the central issues in all relationships—communications about important topics.

General Web Sites:

The American Association for Marriage and Family Therapy's web site at (www.aamft.org/index_nm.asp), although primarily oriented toward professional therapists, provides information on relationship issues and is an excellent source for finding professional help with marriage or other family problems.

The BC Council for Families (www.bccf.bc.ca/) web site is an excellent example of the many local or regional sites providing information and links for those seeking help at the local level. Available in English or French this site also exemplifies the many fine Canadian web sites relevant to the choices facing those in their sixties.

The International Association for Relationship Research (www.iarr.org/) "seeks to stimulate and support the scientific study of personal relationships and encourage cooperation among social scientists worldwide." IARR sponsors two journals, *Personal Relationships* and the *Journal of Social and Personal Relationships.*

Books and Web Sites for Specific Topics:

Friends and Families:

Yager. Jan (1999). *Friendshifts: The Power of Friendship and How It Shapes Our Lives.* Stamford, CT: Hannacroix Creek Books. Both research and practice on making and maintaining friendships are emphasized in this book—including friendships with family members.

McGinnis, A. (1979). *Friendship Factor: How to Get Closer to the People You Care for.* Minneapolis, MN: Augsburg Fortress Press. An inexpensive older classic on the topic of friendship, this book emphasizes the importance of making friendships a top priority if you want a satisfying life. Written from a religious perspective, it includes spousal friendships, friendships between other relatives and other relationships.

The Foundation for Grandparenting's web site (www. grandparenting.org/) offers a variety of information and resources on this topic of central importance to many in their sixties, including help for grandparents who are themselves raising grandchildren. Headed by Arthur Kornhaber, M.D., the foundation sponsors research and training related to healthy grandparenting.

Loss and Death/Bereavement:

The Association for Pet Loss and Bereavement (www.aplb.org/ frame.html) provides comprehensive advice, links and support to those bereaved by loss of a beloved pet.

Growthhouse.Org at (www.growthhouse.org/famgrief.html) is dedicated to improving care for the dying. This comprehensive site deals in depth with death as well as bereavement.

James, J. & Friedman, R. (1998). *The Grief Recovery Handbook: The Action Program for Moving Beyond Death, Divorce, and Other Losses.* N.Y.: HarperCollins. A proven program for recovery from loss and grief is effectively communicated by two leading grief counselors.

McWilliams, P. et al. (1993). *How to Survive the Loss of a Love.* Los Angeles: Mary Book/Prelude Press. This small, inexpensive book deals with recovering from all kinds of lost loves. It is a very practical best seller.

Marriage:

About Marriage (http://marriage.about.com) is an interesting, offbeat web site hosted by Sheri and Bob Stritof, experienced marriage counselors. Information ranges from factual to fanciful on this pleasant and useful site.

Kemp, E, & Kemp, J. (2003). *Older Couples, New Romances: Finding and Keeping Love in Later Life.* Berkeley, CA: Celestial Arts. This inexpensive book is for those desiring to find and keep new love in later life.

Yogev, S. (2001). *For Better or for Worse…But Not for Lunch: Making Marriage Work in Retirement.* N.Y.: McGraw-Hill. This straight forward, common sense book is full of tips on improving marriage after retirement. Self-quizzes for each major topic are included.

Sexual Relations: (Be forewarned: The works below, while not especially prurient, are very concrete and specific about all matters sexual.)

Block, J. & Bakos, S. (1999). *Sex over 50.* Paramus, NJ: Reward Books. Aimed for the boomer generation, this book covers all aspects of sex during later life.

Butler, R. and Lewis, M. (2002). *The New Love and Sex After 60 (revised edition).* N.Y.: Ballantine Books. The newest version of a book first published in 1976, this work by a psychologist and a physician covers both the scientific findings and common sense aspects of sex among people in their sixties. The *Library Journal* calls it "the best all-around sex manual for older adults."

The Kinsey Institute for Research in Sex, Gender, and Reproduction at (http://kinseyinstitute.org) includes information and a great variety of links relating to sexual issues.

Sexual Health InfoCenter (www.sexhealth.org/sexaging/) is a basic site that presents all aspects of sex in a straight forward fashion. It includes two sections on sex and aging.

3

A Time to Work, a Time to Retire—or Both?

Pete Andrews genuinely liked his job. He liked his leisure, too, but he was able to get in plenty of the fishing he loved during his annual vacation plus three-day weekends and the full week between Christmas and New Year's when his company closed. His job as a purchasing agent for an aerospace firm was interesting but not physically demanding. All in all, he really had never thought about retiring. If it ever came up, his image was of something that would happen at 70 or so. Then, when Pete was 55, the bottom fell out of the aircraft industry, and his company began reducing their workforce. Besides laying off some of the "last hired," they offered a generous retirement package to many of their experienced employees, including Pete. He faced a daunting set of questions. Should he take the offer to leave work 15 years earlier than he had expected? Would he and his wife, Harriet, have enough income for the rest of their lives? If Harriet kept on with her career in real estate, would she resent his not working?

Perhaps the choice that most distinguishes the decade of the sixties is this one: deciding when or whether to retire. The decision has significant consequences on how the third stage of life will be lived. Of course, many people have been able to plan their lives so that they can retire before they reach 60. Others have deliberately organized their career so that they can continue pursuing it into their

70s or even longer. Still others must keep working because they can't live on whatever pension and savings they have accumulated, or the decision is made for them when they are laid off or their employer goes out of business. But by originally setting eligibility for full Social Security benefits to begin at 65, our society has branded the sixties as the time to retire, and most Americans do in fact end their working lives sometime during this decade.

Where does "retirement" come from? The modern notion of retirement goes back to the 1880s, when Bismarck created a social support system for Germans. At that time, 90 percent of all 65-year-old American men were still working, a majority of them on farms. Beginning in 1880, according to Dora L. Costa in *The Evolution of Retirement*, the proportion of working men in the total population has declined almost continuously. This is true for all groups—native-and foreign-born, urban and rural, black and white—and for a number of European countries as well as the United States. Since the end of World War II, the decline has been precipitous. It should be noted that Costa's work focuses on men; until recently, she points out, retirement has not been a meaningful concept for women because so few have had lifelong careers.

One factor that led people to retire was the introduction of old-age pensions, replacing the income from work. In 1890, the U.S. Pension Bureau established the first large-scale pension program, for veterans of the Union army. The bureau followed Germany in pegging the retirement age at 65, as most other plans have done since then. This program was the major source of assistance to Americans 65 and older through the early years of the twentieth century. In

1910, one-fourth of the population over 64, both veterans and their dependents, were receiving benefits from this program.

The federal government first adopted a retirement plan for its employees in 1920; most states enacted pension plans, typically limited in scope, during the 1920s and 1930s. American Express created the earliest private pension plan in the United States in 1875, but no more than a dozen private plans existed by 1900. The post-World War II period saw a big boost in such plans, although even by the mid-1980's, less than 50 percent of private wage-and salary-earners were covered.

Until the last 20 years, the majority of private pension plans have been "defined benefit plans," which assure covered workers of a specified monthly benefit after they retire. Such plans are insured by an agency of the federal government, the Pension Benefit Guaranty Corporation (PBGC). By 1985, the PBGC was covering 114,000 defined benefit plans. However, since that time the number of these plans has dropped; in 2003 there were 32,500. What has occurred in the interim is the growth of "defined contribution" plans such as the 401(k). These plans require regular contributions by both employer and employee, with the amount of the pension determined by the value of the funds invested by the time the employee retires. Eighty percent of workers with private pensions were in defined benefit plans in 1980, but by 1998 this had dropped to 45 percent. For 35 percent of workers, 401(k) plans had become the primary plan.

The decline in the stock market starting in 2000 eroded the value of defined contribution plans. At the same time, company losses and bankruptcies threatened the defined benefit plans as well. Although these plans are guaranteed by the government through the PBGC, escalating payouts resulting from bankruptcies and under-funded plans could necessitate reduction in the monthly benefits.

The other major source of support for retirees, of course, is Social Security, created by Congress in 1935. In the beginning it covered a fairly limited number of types of employment, but in 1950, 10 million more workers were covered, and benefits and coverage continued to expand until the late 1970s and early 1980s. According to the Employee Benefit Research Institute, Social Security now provides nearly all of the income for over 40 percent of retired people.

Financial advisers agree, however, that Social Security is "a life preserver, not life support." The experts have always advised people of the need to have their own savings to augment income from Social Security. New Yorker Allan Wikman, who had never stayed on one job long enough to have a pension, is now a 70-year-old living on monthly benefit checks of about $1,000. According to an Associated Press interview, he says, "You can have bare subsistence living on Social Security, but if you don't have savings, you don't have choices." These are his coping strategies: "I rent an apartment from a very accommodating landlady. I don't go to the movies. I don't drink any more. I don't smoke any more. I don't even buy books, but get them from the library. I've learned to do without." In other words, it's possible to scrape by if Social Security is your sole source of retirement income. But your later life can be much more pleasant if you are able to plan your finances to augment your monthly Social Security check. For more information on your Social Security benefits, including recent changes in when you can begin to receive your benefits, see Chapter 6.

What are your options? Still, with support from pensions and Social Security as well as other assets, most Americans in their 60's and older have been able to stop working much earlier than previous generations could. According to a *Newsweek* report, 78 percent of men 60 to 64 and 31 percent of those over 65 were working in 1960. Those figures had changed to 55 and 18 percent respectively by 2000.

People in this age group now are healthier than ever, too. Nowadays people can expect to live 15 to 20 years after retirement—statistically, the average is 17.5 years. Most of them will enjoy active lives during those years if they take care of themselves. Most people today view the idea of retirement positively, a time of increased freedom and opportunity to enjoy life. In fact, Gail Sheehy discovered that among the baby boomers she interviewed for *New Passages*, many hope to retire at 55. The three of us are good examples of this trend. The older two of us, Julie and John, retired voluntarily in our early 60s, and as we finished the first draft of this book, the youngest, Delight, announced her decision to retire at 60.

For lots of reasons, though, working people may choose to postpone retiring. Many can't afford it. Comparing the cost of the life style they enjoy with what they will earn from Social Security and diminishing returns from a 401(k) plan, they decide they will need to keep working. According to *Consumer Reports*, "Anemic retirement savings and the disappearance of pensions may also force people to delay the day they hang up their work duds. Almost 1 in 5 U.S. investors out of 1,001 polled [in 2002] said they planned to postpone their retirement an average of 4.5 years because of the recent market downturn." If they're lucky, they'll be able to keep their health and their job, but not everyone who needs to keep working is so lucky.

Barbara is single, in her late 50's, and unemployed. An independent woman who had worked in information technology, she had always rented a home. Then she was laid off during the dot.com downturn. She expected to be re-hired quickly, but the downturn lasted longer than anyone anticipated. As the economy has improved, plenty of younger people were available for work in her field. Currently her savings are close to being depleted and she still has several years to go before she can draw Social Security. She will have no other pension because for much of her working life she was a contract worker and did not receive retirement benefits. Barbara faces a future that is much more constricted than she had planned.

Others may be financially able to retire but may have an interesting job that they are good at and enjoy, and they see no reason to quit just because they've reached a certain age. Or they may be workaholics who can't imagine what they will do if they retire. They may dread the loss of status and identity their job provides, or they may be attached to their work because they enjoy the personal relationships and social life. Often older workers would like to stay on the job working part-time if that is an option.

This was a choice for Marge Enfield of Shawnee, Ohio, who was featured in a syndicated newspaper story in 2002. At 79, she was still working as a waitress a couple of days a week at Pegah's Family Restaurant, and she said she'd rather be working a couple of days a week than spending time at a senior center. One of her co-workers was quoted as saying, "Sometimes she runs us under the table." Enfield said the social interaction was what kept her working, and her warm and bantering relationship with customers made it clear that interaction was a real energizer for her.

For people who have not been in the workforce and are financially dependent on a partner, the choice is whether and when to encourage the partner to retire. For non-working wives, the questions are how ready they are to down-size their expectations, if that is necessary, and to help in adjusting to this radical change in life rhythm and substance. The growing number of couples waiting until their late 30s and 40s to have children adds a new complication: teen-aged children may also be one of the decision factors.

Tim Williams is an insurance agent who always had an adequate income to support his wife and three daughters. After his divorce, he was able to continue child support until his girls were 18, but it took much of his retirement nest egg. Then in his mid-50s he married a much younger woman, and they had two children together. In his late 60s, he was still supporting two teen-agers. He was also trying to prepare for his retirement and that of his wife, who he anticipated would live longer than he. Although she had a job in a beauty salon, he knew that she would need income to augment Social Security after he died. Needless to say, he chose to continue working on into his 70s.

Of all the choices that face people in their sixties, this one is central: to retire or not to retire. Those who retire face a major transition. For those who decide to keep working, this is still a time to begin preparing for the transition when it does come. All of us face transitions throughout our lives; our goal is to navigate them successfully. Let's look at the opportunities and challenges of the transition from work to retirement.

What are the opportunities? If you have earned a living wage for most of your working life and planned for your future well, you will be able to select when and how you will retire. You can choose whether to simply walk away or to choose a new work configuration or to go into something entirely different. Today, the world of work offers a host of variations from the old convention of the 8-to-5, five-day-a-week job, and the same holds true for retirement. People now often say that they aren't retiring, they're just changing career paths. Not everyone has the freedom to make these choices, but advance planning can increase the degree of control you have over your retirement options.

If you would like to continue working but at a slower pace than your full-time job, one option is to step down to a less demanding rung on your career ladder, recognizing that it may also be less lucrative.

Delight's riding mentor, Hans, is an example of a person who made a complete change in work as he approached his sixties. Brought to the U.S. in the late 1970s as president of a horse breeding farm, which provided a mansion, a high salary, and international-quality horses to work with, over the years he found that the job grew to include sales, auctions, and stallion testing. He moved further and further from training horses and more into management of people. Stresses increased yearly. Demands of the job spilled over into family life. After recognizing that these stresses would not diminish, he and his wife decided to make an abrupt and drastic change. He resigned the position, moved to a different state, and set up a personal business training a few select horses and traveling around the country giving riding clinics. Hans reports that the stresses are different. A regular monthly paycheck is gone, but he controls all decisions and can organize his life as he sees fit. The stress is now challenging and exciting even though he works as hard as he ever did. Now in his mid-sixties, he feels it was the right decision for him and his family.

You may also be able to serve your organization on a contract or consulting basis, providing some specific area of expertise that may be difficult to replace. You might even step up a notch; for example, you may be able to parlay your management experience in a large organization to hire out for interim leadership positions in smaller firms. Or you might be able simply to reduce your time on the job, working shorter days or weeks, or just part of the year.

Andy Hanson spent the better part of his working life as a longshoreman. He eventually worked his way up to a lead position on the docks and was valued for his organizational expertise in managing crews and dock operations. Long divorced, he loved travel, so when he reached retirement age, he looked for a way to continue earning income while indulging his hobby. He was hired by a major city in Southeast Asia to advise them on increasing the efficiency of their cargo operations, and when that six-month stint was done, he had a chance to do the same thing in South America. The work was stimulating, financially rewarding, and enabled him to buy a home on the beach in Peru, where he now spends half the year.

If you are self-employed, you are likely to have considerable flexibility in how you will retire. The kinds of decisions you will make are whether to bring in partners, hire additional skilled people to give yourself more free time, or sell the business with an agreement as to how much longer you want to participate. Julie's husband, Gordon, chose to sell his dental practice outright, taking care to select a dentist he could recommend with confidence to his long-time patients. Several of his friends tapered off by bringing in an associate for one or more years before leaving the practice. In these cases, compatibility with the associate was also important, since dentistry attracts individuals for whom independence is a strong value.

Another option is to make a complete career change. If your work life has been spent within an organization you may find it rewarding to start a small entrepreneurial business, especially if you have Social Security and other pension benefits to cushion the risk. Derek enjoyed repairing and remodeling his own home, so, after 20 years as an electronics technician for an airline, he retired and began a successful second career in home repairs. A life-long gardener, Carolyn opened a boutique nursery after retiring from her career as a school librarian. The Service Corps of Retired Executives (SCORE) partners with the U.S. Small Business Administration to help people start and sustain small businesses. They provide a network of professionals who offer free advice and counseling and would be a good resource if this is your interest.

Training to acquire a new skill is another option. Community and technical colleges are a convenient and economical source of training, both short-and long-term, for many of the careers that are important in your region. You will find that you are not the only non-traditional student going back to school. In many popular community college programs, a majority of the students already have bachelor's degrees and are returning to learn a marketable new skill. Most colleges also offer free career counseling and access to computerized information on job availability in your area.

When Bill retired in his early 60s from his job in information systems for the state of Nevada, he realized that he couldn't maintain the lifestyle he and his wife wanted on his government pension. On the other hand, he didn't want to be tied down again to full-time work year around. By learning to be a tax consultant, he found he could work only a few months a year and still increase his income enough to allow the travel and other activities he and his wife desired.

Then there is real retirement—quitting cold turkey, focusing on other parts of your life. It's for you if you endorse the common saying, "No one ever said on his death bed that he wished he'd spent more time at the office." Time with family and friends, with volunteering, gardening, hobbies, sports, travel—these are the rewards for a lifetime of working, and those who are able to reap them generally express contentment with the retired life. Leisure activities and relationships with family and friends are keys to successful retirement. Retirees may also begin to pay more attention to their health, which is often ignored during the working years, e.g., they eat better, exercise more and so on. Other chapters discuss these matters in depth.

The two of us, Julie and John, who retired in our early 60s, long before we began to write this book, "really" retired. In retrospect, both of us are happy with that decision. It's important to note, as mentioned in the first chapter, that we both have remained very involved with our profession and community through volunteer work, consulting, and writing. Both of us have been accused half-jokingly of not retiring at all but of simply having stopped being paid. Despite that accusation, we both have significantly increased our involvement with our extended families and friends as well.

Considerable research has looked at how well people adjust to retirement. Most studies, *Adult Life* reports, found that in general people adjust well. The majority of those surveyed were satisfied and well adjusted, considered their income adequate and saw no difference in their health in retirement. Blue-collar workers were most satisfied, perhaps because they were happy to leave jobs that were monotonous or physically demanding. African Americans and Hispanics, who were generally less well-off financially, were less satisfied in retirement than other blue-color workers. Professionals and the highly educated react less positively to retirement. As a group they postpone it longest, but once retired, they too adjust well. Across categories, the most satisfied retirees are the ones with the most flexibility as well as the most resources, both financial and social.

Very likely that finding helps explain why all three of us have found the idea of being free during our 60s so appealing. We all have worked hard to assure that we will have adequate financial resources and a broad spectrum of social support during the last third of our lives.

What are the challenges? Not everyone who retires is happy about it. Retirement forced by an employer jolts the ego even if the severance package provides financial security. If a person hasn't worked long enough to have Social Security or another pension, or if she has major expenses such as medical costs or family responsibilities, retirement is not an attractive prospect. Nor is the transition easy for the person whose whole life is wrapped up in her job or the position it gives her. Many women who have come late into the workforce continue working longer than their husbands. This may at least partly be because working has given them a sense of personal accomplishment and an independent social network that wasn't open to them in the days before women's liberation.

Pauline went into real estate sales after her children were grown, and she has developed a group of loyal clients and a referral network that has enabled her to contribute steadily to the family income. She enjoys her work and many of her clients have become friends. When her husband retired, she was not ready to give up either the income or the social relationships her work gives her. Fortunately, she has been able to organize her work life so that she has ample time with her husband and family.

To write *New Passages*, Gail Sheehy surveyed a large group of Stage Three adults (mid-sixties and beyond) and found that adjusting to retirement was tough for many of them. She says professionals and managers put off retiring longest and go back to work more often than other groups. Among the most financially successful subjects, the decade running up to retirement was the low point. They reported being anxious about the loss of identity and status their jobs gave them. Sheehy adds, though, that when she talked with them ten years later, in their mid-sixties, "the men at this stage were happier with their lives than they had *ever* been."

A challenge for the person who chooses to work on past retirement age is to overcome the stereotype, dominant since the days of Bismarck, that people over 60 can't be productive workers. The stereotype is beginning to break down, however. Many researchers have looked at this issue, and the common conclusion is that older workers are valuable workers. One clear sign that attitudes are changing is that the Social Security system has increased the age for receiving benefits. For example, people born in 1960 won't draw full benefits until they are 67. As the large clump of boomers moves toward what was once considered "old age," frequent news stories feature people like Marge Enfield, still working as a waitress at 79, who are successfully continuing on the job or find interesting new work. One source of ideas about good firms to work for is the annual list of the Best Employers for Workers over 50 gathered by the AARP (formerly the American Association of Retired Persons).

Nevertheless, for reasons of physical or mental health, many people do lose the capacity or the enthusiasm to continue working. If they have a good pension or a simplified lifestyle that Social Security benefits can support, they can be happy in retirement. Because you can't be sure how you'll feel about working at 62 or 65, you can't begin retirement planning too soon.

This brings us to one of retirement's major challenges and that is financial. George Vaillant, the author of *Aging Well*, asserts that money is not a factor in successful aging. Still, those retirees who are most dissatisfied are the ones with the least money. Everyone has a different idea of how much money is enough to live on. The important thing is that you figure out what that number is for you and then plan for a retirement income as close to that figure as possible. Chapter 6 on finances will give you ideas on what you need to think about and how to learn more about this.

In general, most people enjoy retirement. They may miss the regular pay-check and their friends at the office, but they usually don't miss their jobs. *Aging Well* notes that among men who took part in a large long-time study, "those who liked working liked retirement." These authors also found that four activities are keys to a rewarding retirement: establishing another social network to replace the one at work; rediscovering how to play, being creative, and continuing to learn. There are many examples of people who follow this advice. A local bookstore's book club was the starting point for a new social network Kathy created for herself after she retired from a retail sales job. Dick, a career electrical engineer, learned to play the viola da gamba and was a regular member of a quartet playing early music on authentic instruments. Al is a psychologist who studied the computer and became expert enough that he now teaches computer classes for seniors. A number of books are devoted to examining the effects of retirement and offering advice on how to prepare for a successful retirement. Several are listed at the end of this chapter.

Adult Life tells us, "There appears to be no universal best way to retire." Retirement is as individual as every other aspect of your career life. If you like to plan and don't like surprises, you'll want to spend some quality time looking at what's best for you in retiring—how much money you'll need, how much you'll miss the challenge and status of work, what kind of social life you have or can muster away from the workplace. If on the other hand you've always changed jobs impulsively and happily, you may one day just up and quit, confident you can float like a butterfly through the changes that retirement brings. It's up to you to choose your own best way.

RESOURCES

Books:

The first two books provide a broad look at aspects of retirement. The others are examples of the many offerings that give advice on ways to approach retirement to create the most satisfaction with this time in your life.

Costa, D. (1998). *The Evolution of Retirement: An American Economic History, 1880-1990.* Chicago: University of Chicago Press. This is a scholarly but readable account of retirement trends using statistical and demographic data. It also anticipates further evolution of retirement including such issues as the impact of baby boomers on the Social Security System.

Freedman, M. (2002). *Prime Time: How Baby Boomers Will Revolutionize Retirement and Transform America.* New York: Public Affairs, LLC. Freedman proposes that the nation and its citizens will benefit if the rapidly growing older population is recognized as a significant social resource.

Anthony, M. (2001). *The New Retirementality: Planning Your Life and Living Your Dreams...At Any Age You Want.* Chicago: Dearborn Trade Publishing. Anthony proposes an alternative to the traditional view of retirement, proposing that "flexible, phased retirement" may be a better model.

Autry, J. (2002). *The Spirit of Retirement: Creating a Life of Meaning and Personal Growth.* Roseville, CA: Prima Publishing. This book offers ways to make the transition to retirement fulfilling, illustrated with anecdotes and exercises for the reader.

Grace, R. (2002). *When Every Day Is Saturday: The Retirement Guide for Boomers.* Lincoln, Nebraska: iUniverse, Incorporated. This how-to book is based on a study of 700 retirees and uses the results to advise how to plan for a happy and meaningful retirement.

Rich, P., et al. (1999). *The Healing Journey Through Retirement.* New York: John Wiley & Sons. The authors provide a guide for exploring the meaning of work and plans for the period after leaving the work force to make a satisfying transition to the retirement years.

Smith, M. & Smith S. (1999). *The Retirement Sourcebook.* Los Angeles: Lowell House. This book offers practical advice and information on all aspects of retirement as well as a list of organizational resources, including national associations and federal and state agencies.

Warner, R.. (2002) *Get a Life: You Don't Need a Million to Retire Well (4th edition).* Berkeley, CA: Nolo.com. Warner writes that financial planning is only one of the important aspects of successful retirement and identifies activities, options and ways of organizing your life to retire happily even if you haven't put away large sums of money.

Web Sites:

AARP (formerly the American Association of Retired Persons) (www.aarp.org) lists their selection of the Best Employers for Workers over 50.

Center for Creative Retirement (www.unca.edu/ncccr) is one of 18 centers, sponsored by colleges or universities in 11 states and the province of Manitoba, that involve older adults in "lifelong learning, personal enrichment, community service, and intergenerational activities." This site provides links to the other centers.

Employee Benefit Research Institute (www.ebri.org) is a nonprofit organization that disseminates data and carries out policy research and education on economic security and employee benefits.

Pension Benefit Guaranty Corporation (www.pbgc.gov) provides thorough information on defined benefit pension plans.

The Retirement Research Foundation (www.rrf.org) sponsors research through its network of individuals and institutions focused on aging and retirement issues.

Service Corps of Retired Executives (www.score.org) connects you with a national network of volunteer business executives and professionals who advise and counsel business start-ups. You may find this site useful if you want to access their services or to volunteer yourself.

Social Security Administration (www.ssa.gov) is the site for all inquiries regarding Social Security—history and current status of the system and answers to all kinds of questions about benefits.

U.S. Department of Labor (www.dol.gov) offers America's Job Bank, a listing service for employers and employees, and Occupational Outlook Handbook, giving information on specific occupations, what they entail and what the job prospects are.

4

Is Physical Health a Matter of Choice?

When asked if he would like to live to 90 or 100, Chris Adamson, who had just turned 60, replied, "Sure, as long as I'm healthy at that age. Wouldn't it be great to see my great-grandkids grow up?" Like Chris, nearly all people say they wish to enjoy long lives but realize that enjoying the last third of life requires remaining functionally healthy—both physically and mentally. The question, then, is whether those in their 60s can do anything to help assure a healthy last third of their lives or whether it is too late to make any difference. The good news is that recent research on aging shows definitively that the right health choices made in your 50s and 60s can pay huge dividends later. The bad news is that wrong choices can lead to sickly aging and premature death.

The contrast in health during their sixties and beyond between John's parents and Delight's parents shows how choices made during and before your sixth decade can make a huge difference. John's father George, who has been dead since 1980, never had a really healthy day after 65 even though he survived to 75. John's mother, Perpetua, died at 67 four years before his father. Conversely, at this writing Delight's parents are in their early nineties and have been in good health until very recently.

The premature ill health and deaths of John's parents did not result from bad genes. Perpetua's father died at 82 of prostate cancer while her mother, who bore sixteen children and raised eight, lived to 74 despite being a severe diabetic. George's father, who had been in excellent health, died from a botched prostate surgery at 78, and his mother lived to 84, having raised four children. The health differences between generations clearly resulted from life-style choices, not heredity.

George smoked heavily from age ten until a near-death episode when he was 65 prompted his doctor to tell him, "You can smoke and die or give it up and live—your choice." Being a person who loved life, he finally quit. Because he had done physical work all his adult life and had controlled his weight, the doctors said he no doubt would have lived many more years in good health except that he had ruined his lungs. Even though he quit smoking, the damage already done finally killed him after several more years of illness interspersed with brief good periods.

Perpetua hadn't smoked until she met George at age 21, but once having started she continued until she dropped dead from a heart attack at 67 just after finishing her last cigarette. In addition to smoking heavily, Perpetua never exercised and was very overweight most of her adult life until about a year before her death when she suddenly lost a great deal of weight. And, most likely, she was a closet diabetic, which she partially controlled by diet. Her children, all of whom lived in other cities, learned after her death that as her health declined while she took care of George, she never once went to the doctor herself.

The sadness caused by John's parents' premature deaths was doubled when both his mother-in-law and father-in-law died at 61 and

67, respectively. They too were heavy smokers who rarely exercised and ate the classic meat, potatoes, gravy and dessert most every day.

Delight's parents followed a different path. Both were smokers when young, but when her grandfather died of lung cancer, both quit in their 40s. Her father retired early and together her parents planned and oversaw the production of a sailboat. They spent the next twenty years taking paying guests around the Caribbean, Europe, and finally the east coast. As Delight's father Bob reached 75, he decided he was too old to sail like that, so he took a final trip—from Maine to Nova Scotia to the Azores then to the Canary Islands, the Cape Verdes and back across the Atlantic to Venezuela, and finally across the Caribbean to Florida. But after enjoying that adventure they decided to ship the boat to the Pacific Northwest and continued sailing for another five years, until he reached 80. Finally the boat was sold.

This active life kept both vitally involved physically and mentally. Exploration of Greek ruins while they spent time on the Turkish coast led to an ongoing fascination with archeology that continues to this day.

Delight's mother, now in her nineties, has had both hips replaced plus one surgery for cancer, but she continues to be active with family and friends. Delight's father, just turning 90, has been diagnosed with terminal bone cancer. He is facing this with his usual energy. "No one is immortal, and I have had a great life," is his attitude. He has hosted two meetings with his wife, children and his doctor to discuss his end-of-life wishes. The doctor has repeatedly said how wonderful it is to have an open discussion with all involved before a crisis. "If only more families could face these questions openly!" is his constant comment.

In this chapter we discuss the choices leading to good physical health and in the next chapter those involved in maintaining good mental functioning. Separating physical and mental health this way is useful for discussion, but all the recent research shows huge overlaps between them. Those with excellent mental health often lead full, happy lives despite significant physical problems, while people who make the right choices to upgrade their physical health usually see improved mental functioning as well. When the right choices are made, it is not uncommon to find a person healthier at 69 than she or he was at 59 when the pressures of every day life made finding time to maintain health more difficult.

So, what choices need to be made during your 60s concerning your physical health:

- What will you eat?

- To drink or not to drink alcohol?

- What kind of exercise routine will you follow?

- Is "use it or lose it" really true?

- To smoke or not to smoke?

- Are there pills you should or shouldn't take?

- Immunizations you should or shouldn't have?

- When, if ever, should you go to the doctor?

- Do you still need to floss in your 60s?

- What about the really scary things such as heart disease, cancer, stroke and Alzheimer's disease; can your choices do anything about them?

- Won't your body decay no matter what you do, and, if so, how much does decaying really matter in everyday life?

What will you eat? The old saying, "You are what you eat," contains a great deal of truth according to modern research on healthy aging. For example, David Snowdon, Ph.D., the author of *Living with Grace: What the Nun Study Teaches Us about Leading Healthier and More Meaningful Lives* and a leading expert on Alzheimer's disease, says, "So while scientists bob and weave through the thicket of dietary research, it may be that heaping our plates at the salad bar…is our best nutritional strategy for warding off aging and Alzheimer's disease."

Similarly, in reporting on the landmark Harvard Study of Adult Development George Vaillant shares "seven protective factors" characteristic of middle-aged people who remained healthy into their late 70s and beyond. Two of the seven factors relate to eating—no alcohol abuse and not being overweight. Interestingly, this study did not find cholesterol level, another food-related factor commonly thought to affect healthy aging, to be predictive.

As if to reinforce these findings of the Nun Study and the Harvard longitudinal study, Thomas Perls, M.D., and Margery Hutter Silver, Ed.D. recently reported that among the centenarians they studied in New England, 99 percent "did not meet the criteria for obesity" and none of the centenarians reported having abused alcohol. As they note in *Living to 100: Lessons in Living to Your Maximum Potential at Any Age,* "about 80 percent of centenarians said that their current weight was close to what they had weighed for their entire adult lives."

These three well-done and well-known studies exemplify what researchers increasingly say—choices about what and how much you eat and drink matter greatly. If we really want to remain healthy in the last third of our lives—to avoid or eliminate obesity, to avoid or reduce the effects of diabetes, high blood pressure, heart disease, stroke, and cancer—the type of foods we eat, the amount of food and drink we consume, the supplementary vitamins and minerals we use, and the way we use alcoholic beverages can make a great difference. Let's look at what research says about each of these.

During the twentieth century each generation reached its 60s healthier and with a longer life expectancy than its predecessor—an amazing achievement. However, a recent trend to obesity among younger people has experts wondering whether we are about to reverse that century-long trend. Aside from avoiding starvation, nothing good comes from being obese. On the contrary nearly every negative health factor is made worse by excess weight: diabetes rates explode upward, arthritis increases, heart disease skyrockets, etc. Thus, choices about weight control matter a great deal.

The basic formula for attaining and maintaining a healthy weight is simple enough: *eat less, exercise more, do it forever*. But, if you have given it a moment's thought, you know that. The real problem for many comes in doing what they know they should. Here knowing yourself and what motivates you is critical. If the details of how to proceed present a problem, see one of the books or web sites on diet in the reference section at the end of the chapter. If you know you can't do it alone, join a support group. If you have physical or mental problems creating a barrier to attaining a healthy weight, see your physician or mental health counselor right away. Choosing in your 60s to attain and maintain a healthy weight often means choosing to permanently alter your lifestyle. Since the alternatives are sickness and/or early death, the choice should be clear even if implementing it is harder.

Although less important than controlling excess weight, what you eat and when and how you eat it also matter. Unfortunately, however, studies in this area tend to ambiguity and even contradiction. You will want to stay tuned as this research develops, but for now the following seem safe choices. Eating smaller quantities more often works better than the traditional "three squares." Emphasizing a variety of fruit and vegetables in your diet clearly pays dividends as does avoiding excess animal fat. Daily, consume the equivalent of eight or more glasses of water or other liquid. Beyond these, you need to eat and drink a variety of foods that provide the vitamins and minerals your body needs for health. If you have any doubt as to whether you are getting them in your diet, consider taking a multi-vitamin daily—also see the discussion below on diet supplements. Several of the items in the chapter resources contain excellent summaries on balancing your diet.

In *Aging with Grace* Dr. Snowdon reminds us that choices we make about the social side of eating also matter: "What I know for sure is that healthy nutrition for healthy aging is not just about eating certain foods or downing a certain number or milligrams of a prescribed number of vitamins each day. It also depends on where we eat, whom we eat with, and whether the meal nourishes our heart, mind, and soul as well as our body."

Each of us has taken a different approach to diet. John has the good fortune of being married to a superb cook who is also an expert on healthful nutrition, so a balanced diet has always been the norm at their house. Beyond that, he has learned he is better at avoiding than resisting calorie-rich sweets. Julie's good fortune was something she didn't appreciate when she was young: her mother was a "health-food nut" long before it was the fashion. At least partly in consequence, Julie has always been healthy, and she eventually came to accept her mother's wisdom. In fact, their grown children still consider her and her dentist husband as having been over the top in insisting on a nutritious and relatively sugar-free diet. The vindication is that all four grown children are still free of dental caries. Delight, on the other hand, has always faced a weight problem. Dieting is more or less constant, with intense efforts followed by times when she decides not to care, but to eat carefully. Then the weight comes on again. It's a frustrating challenge, because she stays active, exercising by usually riding one to two horses daily, and doesn't eat sweets, but she is, in horse terms, "an easy keeper."

To drink or not to drink alcohol? Unlike the research on many other aspects of diet, studies on the inclusion of alcohol in the diet are clear. Alcohol abuse affects health severely and negatively and, like obesity, must be avoided or stopped if you hope for a healthy final third of you life. On the other hand, if abuse is not a problem, moderate use of alcohol does not harm health and, according to some studies, may even improve it.

In *Aging Well* Dr. Vaillant reports that of the seven factors in late middle age that predicted physical and mental health in the 70s and 80s, only absence of alcohol abuse "powerfully predicted both psychosocial and physical health." His summary of several long-term studies about alcohol abuse should eliminate any doubt about the need to choose to deal with it: "Prospective study reveals that alcohol abuse is a *cause* rather than a result of increased life stress, of depression, and of downward social mobility. In addition alcohol abuse causes death for many reasons other than liver cirrhosis and motor vehicle accidents. Alcohol abuse causes suicide, homicide, cancer, heart disease, and a depressed immune system."

Harry drank heavily for many years before retiring. He took some pride in always being able to keep the job he loved despite his addiction. Once he retired "to enjoy some time with the grandkids," he discovered that neither they nor his children had much desire to be around him when he had been drinking, which was most of the time. One day he overheard his favorite grandson tell his sister to "stay away from Grandpa. He's drunk again." The next day he attended his first AA meeting and began the struggle to put his life together again.

If you have an alcohol abuse problem and want to have a healthy last third of your life, your choice is clear. Choose to stop. Again, as with obesity, the best way for you to deal with such a problem will vary with your personality, environment and resources. Many, perhaps most, will need help staying sober. Fortunately, help is only an AA meeting or a phone call away. See the chapter resources under alcohol abuse for suggestions. People who care deeply about you and your health are always available.

For those without an abuse problem, the choices are simpler—to drink those two glasses of red wine each day or not. Some research in recent years seems to show positive health effects from moderate alcohol consumption, although the studies vary on whether specific types of drinks matter. And, very recently, a large study seems to have shown that the life style followed by people who drink wine in moderation actually makes the difference. Again, stay tuned for further studies, all of which should be taken with a grain of salt. What seems certain at this point is that alcohol taken in moderation does not, in itself, harm health and may even help. Clearly, however, other things such as exercise matter a lot more.

What kind of exercise routine will you follow?—*and*—**Is "use it or lose it" really true?** It is true! Research has shown that "use it or lose it" applies to many aspects of aging, including physical and mental health. We will look at the mental heath aspects of exercise later. Here we'll examine how exercise improves physical health.

Gail Sheehy says in *New Passages: Mapping Your Life Across Time*, "Exercise appears to be the single most effective nonmedical elixir to retard aging." Then she adds, "Long daily walks are part of the job of successful aging."

As if to reinforce this, when he is asked what is the first thing a person should do to age successfully, Dr. Snowdon, who led the Nun Studies, says he always answers, "Walk." He adds: "Walking is a great exercise for almost everyone. But I also say that the key point is to find some sport or activity that you truly enjoy, so that you will do it regularly—at least four days a week for the rest of your life. This not only protects your heart and bones; it also protects your brain."

And, as mentioned earlier, the Harvard Study of Adult Development found getting at least some exercise in late middle age was one of the seven factors that predict good health 20 years later. So, what does "some exercise" mean to a person in her or his 60s?

In part it means denying a long-held myth that massive decline in muscle mass and strength inevitably resulted from aging itself. For example some earlier studies had shown that between the ages of 20 and 70 people typically lost 40 percent of their muscle mass and 30 percent of their strength—and after 70 things got much worse. We now know that the bulk of this loss came from lack of exercise—a sedentary life style. We sent our muscles—including our heart—the message that they weren't much needed any more, so they just began fading away. Fortunately, recent studies show it's never too late to send a correcting message through exercise.

Basically, exercise falls into two categories—aerobic exercise, which primarily strengthens the cardio-vascular system, and resistance exercise, designed primarily to increase muscle mass and "guard against age-related loss of muscle tissue," as Perls and Silver put it in *Living to 100*. Walking, swimming, jogging, biking, dancing, and the kind of exercises often done to music following a live instructor or videotape typify aerobic exercise. Weight lifting, stair climbing, hill climbing, and numerous activities done in home or commercial gyms with weights or elastic cords exemplify resistance exercise. A balance of both types contributes to good health in many ways.

Regular exercise has been proven to strengthen bones, reduce the risk of falls, and increase muscle mass which, in turn, burns calories much more effectively than fat and aids in weight loss and reduction of obesity. Exercise strengthens the immune system, prevents or delays diabetes and, where Type 2 diabetes is present, it improves glucose control. Still other benefits include reducing the risk of heart disease and improving recovery chances when heart problems do occur, improving sleep patterns, reducing cholesterol levels, and even reducing the incidence of high blood pressure and strokes. As if these were not enough reasons to choose to exercise, the Nun Studies have shown that by preventing strokes—even minor ones—you also dramatically reduce the chance of Alzheimer's causing dementia, even where the plaques and tangles of Alzheimer's are already present.

Unfortunately, in the past getting regular exercise seems not to have been common among those in middle age and beyond. Perls and Silver report data from the US and Canada showing that only 10 percent of those over 65 and only 35 percent of the middle-aged baby boomers do vigorous exercise regularly. In other words, the great majority of North Americans enter the last third of their lives needing to change their exercise regimen if they are to avoid being among the "sad sick" or "prematurely dead," to use the Harvard Study terms. Remember, studies show that every little bit of exercise helps!

In the process of choosing an exercise regimen, persons in their 60s should start with a thorough physical exam and a discussion with their doctors. Beyond that, those with disabilities or who feel insecure designing their own exercise plan can consult with physical therapists or professional fitness planners who are often connected to commercial gyms or senior center services. Your doctor and fitness planners can help you design an exercise program suited to your health and lifestyle while helping you avoid activities that might actually worsen your health. For example, some high impact exercises could bring on or worsen arthritis, which is by far the most common chronic health problem among those 65 or older.

The three of us follow quite different exercise regimens as a result of our differing interests, health, and physical limitations. Julie takes weekly ski lessons each winter—from an instructor who is in his mid-80s—so she walks and does leg-strengthening exercises daily year-round. She has added weight-bearing exercises (plus more cal-cium-rich foods and supplements) to stem encroaching arthritis and osteopenia, the pre-cursor to osteoporosis. John was fortunate enough to reach and pass through his sixties in good health—aside from the prostate cancer treatment mentioned earlier. Throughout his sixties he walked a mile or two daily in hilly Seattle, and until his cancer treatment he often biked several times a week. His volunteer work managing a food bank and dinner for the homeless has pro-vided good resistance exercise several days each week. In fact, he claims to be physically stronger now than at any time since he left the army in his twenties. For some time, Delight walked two miles each way to work up and down the steep hills in downtown Seattle. This helped her weight problem, but probably was the immediate cause of her very rapid hip degeneration. Now she rides regularly and is very active around the horses, but recognizes that an addi-tional exercise regime would be useful. The hip problem makes it hard; perhaps swimming could be an answer. As she moved toward retirement, finding time for more exercise was a goal.

To smoke or not to smoke? Don't smoke! If you do smoke, choose to quit! On this more than any other aspect of healthy living, every expert, every book, every web site on health agrees.

Typical of the research on smoking and health was the finding of the Harvard longitudinal study where the absence of heavy smoking in middle age turned out to be "the most important single predictive factor of healthy physical aging." And while it clearly helps more if you never smoked or quit before middle age, stopping smoking at any age has significant health benefits even though not all the harm done by years of smoking can ever be totally undone.

If you smoke and realize it's time to stop, see the chapter resources for guidance on how to accomplish this critical if difficult task. One thing in your favor is that all health organizations, for both health and financial reasons, recognize the importance of reducing smoking; therefore they commonly offer a variety of free or low-cost helps in this matter. Group Health Cooperative, to which John belongs, is typical. As part of their anti-smoking program, they offer telephone counseling, written materials, two web sites, and a comprehensive, nationally available program called Free & Clear. Free & Clear is described as "tailored to your schedule and needs. You may choose the individual or group program." See www.freeclear.com/ghc/on the web for further information on this program at Group Health or go to www.freeclear.com/ for general information on the national program.

Are there pills you should or shouldn't take? Yes. First, unless you are certain you are regularly eating a well balanced diet, taking a multivitamin daily is probably a wise choice. Recently because of concern that many people of every age eat inadequate diets, the American Medical Association supported the wisdom of everyone taking a multivitamin daily. And Dr. Snowdon, as a result of what he learned from the Nun Studies, follows that practice as well.

Given what he knows about aging, Snowdon also takes a vitamin E antioxidant supplement daily. Similarly, based on their studies of centenarians and aging in general, which show that free oxygen "radicals" in the body contribute to nearly every major health problem, Perls and Silver say, "Diligent use of these antioxidants [vitamin E and selenium], and others yet to be discovered, is our best chance right now to arrest or slow diseases of aging." Perls and Silver also warn that "many multivitamins contain iron and copper, which…may actually speed the rate of oxygen radical damage." The arguments and expertise of Snowdon, Perls, and Silver sufficed initially to convince one of the authors, John, who has always been an anti-pill person, to choose to take 400 IU of vitamin E daily. However, more recent research has called these benefits into doubt and even shown some negative effects, so he no longer takes extra vitamin E. This is another good example of the importance of keeping in touch with the ongoing research related to health issues.

Some research has also shown that taking an aspirin daily or even every other day may reduce the risk of heart attack. If your doctor agrees, this may also a good choice to make unless you have a medical reason not to, such as stomach problems or asthma. Taking the enteric-coated 81 mg. version helps avoid the potential side effects, although some recent research has questioned the effectiveness of coated, reduced-dosage aspirin.

Certainly, many other pills, herbs and diet supplements should be taken by some individuals where health conditions call for them and where research has verified their safety and effectiveness. However, expert advice should always be sought in such matters! Talk with your physician, dietician, or other health professional before choosing. Taking the wrong pills or herbs or diet supplements at the wrong time can do great harm, so better safe than sorry. A warning: Be wary of quacks; they abound in this area.

What about immunizations? Unfortunately, as late as the mid-1990s only about half of Americans 65 and older had annual influenza vaccinations and over two-thirds had failed to get the once-in-a-lifetime inoculation against bacterial pneumonia. One of the reasons so few people have taken the important inoculation against pneumonia seems to be lack of awareness that such a vaccine exists. Therefore, since a great deal of research continues in attempts to develop new vaccines, even for diseases such as AIDS and cancer, you also need to be alert for newly developed vaccines relevant to those 60 and up.

Barring some medical or philosophical reason not to do so, people in their 60s clearly should choose to have both the pneumonia and influenza immunizations. Doing so will prevent a great deal of illness and many premature deaths. The only other immunization currently recommended for everyone over 60 is a tetanus booster every ten years. As to other inoculations—e.g., before traveling to areas where diseases such yellow fever exist—they need to be considered on a case-by-case basis in consultation with your physician and other medical professionals.

When, if ever, should you go to the doctor? For everyone 60 and up, a general physical every few years can uncover conditions while they are still treatable. Such a physical also should provide a chance to ask for any health advice you feel you need. It also gives your general practitioner the opportunity to refer you to a specialist in cases where problems seem to be developing, e.g., for hearing or visual tests which are commonly needed for those in their 60s and above.

Included in or in addition to the scheduled general physical, you should choose to have several other preventive checks on a planned basis. As research continues, preventive services schedules have varied somewhat from time to time and agency to agency. Nonetheless, such schedules can provide guidance to you in deciding how to plan to protect your health.

For example, Group Health Cooperative, a health maintenance organization in Washington state, recommends the following schedule for those 65 and above: Visit your doctor at least every two years for a general physical. Receive immunizations to flu annually, to tetanus-diphtheria every ten years, to pneumonia once after 65, and, if at high risk, to hepatitis B. Women should have a mammogram every one to two years depending on individual risk factors, and men should discuss prostate cancer screening with their doctor. Both men and women should have their blood pressure and stools checked every two years and have a sigmoidoscopy exam for colon cancer every ten years. For those aged 50 to 64 the immunizations for flu and pneumonia are recommended only for those at high risk, and a check of cholesterol every five years for everyone plus a pap test for women every two to three years are added to the schedule.

And, obviously, you should choose to see your doctor when injured or when symptoms of specific health problems appear, e.g., unusual chest pains, new unexplained lumps in a breast or elsewhere, a severe headache that stays on, an infection or sore that fails to heal normally, old blood in the stool, or continuing pain when urinating.

Yes, see your doctor when called for, but remember, you, not your doctor, must make the key decisions about your health. Think of your doctor as an advisor, not as the person in control. Ask questions, ask "why?" Share information, don't hesitate to ask for a second opinion where you have doubts. And do some research yourself, e.g., see some of the health web sites recommended in the chapter resources or read from one or more of the books listed there such as

Healthwise for Life: A Self-care Manual for Older Adults, a wonderful general guide distributed by Group Health Cooperative.

Do you still need to floss in your 60s? Yes, and for reasons beyond the obviously important purpose of keeping your teeth healthy and useful for eating things such as crunchy fruits and vege-tables for the next 20 to 30 years. Research shows that proper tooth care prevents bacterial infections from forming in the mouth and gums. Preventing such gum disease is critical because those infec-tions—and similar low-grade infections elsewhere in the body—have recently been shown to lead often to serious heart dis-ease. All in all, good dental and mouth care positively affect both physical health and your self-perception—both of which are impor-tant to healthy aging.

What about the really scary things such as heart disease, can-cer, stroke and Alzheimer's disease; can your choices do any-thing about them? Their recent bouts with cancer have made Delight and John doubly aware that concern over illnesses such as these makes good sense because they are the major killers and dis-ablers among those in their 60s and beyond. According to data in *Older Americans 2000: Key Indicators of Well-Being,* compiled by the Federal Interagency Forum on Aging Related Statistics, overall, the six top killers in 1997, in order, were heart disease; cancer; stroke; chronic obstructive pulmonary disease (COPD, where breathing is partially blocked, results almost entirely from smoking-caused chronic bronchitis and/or emphysema); pneumonia and influenza; and diabetes. With the exception of American Indians and Alaska Natives where diabetes jumped to third, the top three killers—heart, cancer, and stroke—were the same for men and women and for all races, with heart and cancer deaths being by far the most common for every category. Unintentional injuries, nephritis (kidney failure), Alzheimer's disease, septicemia (systemic infection), hypertension, chronic liver disease and cirrhosis, and atherosclerosis complete the lists of top ten causes of death among various racial groups and men and women, although their order varied considerably within categories.

Other data from the same publication imply that in recent years people have been making better choices about preventing heart disease and stroke, both of which declined by about a third from 1980 to 1997 as a cause of death among those 65 and older. On the other hand, they seem to have been making poor lifestyle choices in relation to cancer, which has risen slightly as a cause of death over that period. More importantly, the same is true in regard to diabetes and chronic obstructive pulmonary diseases, which increased 32 and 57 percent, respectively, in those 17 years.

As we have seen earlier most, if not all, of these leading causes of death among those in their 60s and beyond definitely can be affected by choices concerning diet and vitamins, exercise, smoking, drinking, immunizations, dental care, following a good preventive schedule, and seeking professional health care when appropriate.

Yes, sometimes no matter what good choices you make some of these "scary things" will hit you, and, sooner or later, something will affect you mortally. Nonetheless, the choices you make about your physical health and your mental attitude toward life and health can result in your being one of the "sad-sick" or "prematurely dead" or they can dramatically increase the odds of your living a long, healthy life. Beyond making basic positive health choices, you should learn the specific nature, symptoms, and preventive measures for the top three or four killers plus any of the others that seem relevant to your heredity, lifestyle or health history.

Won't your body decay no matter what you do, and, if so, how much does decaying really matter in every day life? Yes, for now and the foreseeable future your body will decay no matter what you do. However, as we've seen above, you have a great deal of control over the rate and type of decay. In *Adult Life* Judith Stevens-Long and Michael Commons have a number of things to say about decline and decay: "Almost all elderly people notice changes in their skin and bones, but similar processes go on in every other tissue as well. Loss of weight and stiffening occur in every organ and organ system, and these internal changes often affect health and vigor." They continue, "After the age of sixty, most people notice sharp declines in vision and hearing...Although not as noticeable to most people, gustation and olfaction also decline.... Taste buds are lost with age. So are sensory cells in the nose." But then they add this important point: "The question is, are such changes inevitable?...In a society where people take better care of themselves, exercise their abilities, and stay involved with the world around them, no doubt fewer sensory and perceptual changes will occur." In other words, they verify again that "using it" will eliminate or at least delay many of the negatives formerly assumed to be the inevitable result of normal aging.

Drs. Perls and Silver believe one of the most important things proven by their study of the very old is that "growing older does not necessarily mean growing sicker." Sadly, they also point out that "unfortunately, the vast majority of baby boomers do a terrible job of preparing for old age. High-fat diets, smoking, excessive drink-ing, and lack of exercise not only reduce people's chances of achiev-ing older age, they markedly increase the likelihood of a longer period of poor health in a shorter life." Fortunately, as we have seen above, during our 60s transition we have the freedom to choose to be as healthy as our genes and our circumstances allow us to be. Or as Dr. Vaillant puts it in *Aging Well,* "Ultimately, and most bluntly, successful aging means the mastery of decay." In other words, you can master it or decay will master you.

As mentioned earlier, maintaining your physical health during the last third of life has a close relationship to your mental health, which we turn to in the next chapter.

RESOURCES

The following are examples of the hundreds of general books and web sites that cover every topic in this chapter. Most of them also provide guidance or links to even more detailed information on spe-cific topics. Remember, none of these can replace consultation with your health-care provider.

Books:

Mettler, M & Kemper, D. (1992). *Healthwise for Life: Medical Self-Care for Healthy Aging.* Boise, ID: Healthwise Incorporated. This self-care manual for older adults, which is distributed by Group Health Cooperative and other organizations, addresses health issues in plain English and large type. It's an excellent place to start because it's both comprehensive in scope and easy to understand. However, it does not go into depth on most topics.

The following six books are similar to one another in intent and content. Most are comprehensive, contain sections on senior health care, and are reasonably priced. In fact, the 1620 page *Merck Manual* and the 620 page *Physicians' Desk Reference* sell for under $10 while the others typically sell for $30 to $50.

Berkow, R. (ed.) (1999). *The Merck Manual of Medical Information: Home Edition.* N.Y.: Pocket Books.

Clayman, C. (ed.) (1994). *American Medical Association Family Medical Guide (3rd edition).* N.Y.: Random House.

Golman, D. (ed.) (1999). *American College of Physicians Complete Home Medical Guide.* N.Y.: DK Publishing.

Komaroff, A., et al. (1999). *Harvard Medical School Family Health Guide.* N.Y.: Simon and Schuster.

Larson, D., et al. (1997). *Mayo Clinic Family Health Book: the Ultimate Home Medical Reference (2nd edition).* N.Y.: William Morrow & Co.

The Physicians' Desk Reference (editors) (1999). *The Physicians' Desk Reference Family Guide to Medical Care.* N.Y.: Ballantine Books.

Web Sites:

In 2002 the Medical Library Association rated the following web sites as the top general health related sites. *Web addresses may vary over the years,* so if one does not work, a new address can usually be found by searching for the parent organization, e.g., the National Library of Medicine in the first listing.

MEDLINEplus (www.nlm.nih.gov/medlineplus) of the National Library of Medicine, part of the National Institute of Health is current and comprehensive with a vast number of relevant links.

Centers for Disease Control and Prevention (www.cdc.gov), sponsored by the Federal Centers for Disease Control and Prevention, is also comprehensive and current and contains sections on travel and on older adults. It is available in English and Spanish.

Healthfinder (www.healthfinder.gov), sponsored by the Office of Disease Prevention and Health Promotion of the U.S. Department of Health and Human Services, also has a Spanish version and a special section for seniors.

HealthWeb (www.healthweb.org), sponsored by the Greater Midwest Region of the National Network of Libraries of Medicine, provides a vast range of reliable links to health information on every imaginable topic.

HIV InSite (http://hivinsite.ucsf.edu/InSite) concentrates on HIV/AIDS. The University of California San Francisco sponsors this comprehensive world-wide look at every aspect of the HIV/AIDS epidemic.

Mayo Clinic (www.mayoclinic.com/index.cfm), obviously sponsored by the famed Mayo Clinic, offers a superb variety of approaches to learning about health issues. Hundreds of medical schools, HMOs, research sites, and private clinics offer similar sites.

MEDEM (www.medem.com/MedLB/medlib_entry.cfm) is sponsored by several medical organizations including the American Medical Association. It provides access to 44 professional association libraries. It also provides links that allow you to consult online with medical personnel for a fee.

National Women's Health Information Center (www.4women.gov), sponsored by the National Office on Women's Health of the U.S. Department of Health and Human Services, covers in English and Spanish health issues of special importance to women. Excellent links to organizations and publications are included.

NOAH: New York Online Access to Health (www.noah-health.org) is sponsored by a group of New York area public and medical school libraries. Offering both Spanish and English versions, this site provides comprehensive information. It exemplifies the many health sites sponsored throughout the world by health agencies, libraries, and public health offices.

Below are written material and web sites relating to the specific topics discussed in the chapter. Because all of these topics are also covered in the general books and web sites listed above, only a few key resources are included here.

Alcohol Abuse:

Alcoholics Anonymous (www.alcoholics-anonymous.org/), available in Spanish and French as well as English, provides general information and basic materials for those with alcohol problems. Links and/or phone numbers are provided to many local AA groups.

Al-Anon and Alateen (www.al-anon.alateen.org/) provide support for those whose loved ones have problems with alcohol. The site includes general information on the topic as well as contact information for local support groups.

Ketchum, K., et al. (2000). *Beyond the Influence: Understanding and Defeating Alcoholism.* N.Y.: Bantam, Doubleday, Dell Publishers. Based on science, this inexpensive book provides specific valid information and help for those struggling with alcoholism and for their loved ones.

Alzheimer's Disease:

The Alzheimer's Association (www.alz.org/) is a national network of chapters. As the largest national voluntary health organization, it is dedicated to advancing research on Alzheimer's and helping those with the disease.

Mace, N. & Rabins, P. (2001). *The 36-Hour Day: A Family Guide to Caring for Persons with Alzheimer Disease, Related Dementing Illnesses, and Memory Loss in Later Life (revised edition).* N.Y.: Warner Books. This inexpensive book both aids individuals and families in understanding dementia and provides specific advice for those caring for loved ones suffering from this disease.

Cancer:

Oncolink (www.oncolink.upenn.edu), sponsored by the University of Pennsylvania Abramson Cancer Center, provides easily accessed and understood content on all types of cancer and treatment.

Treatment Guidelines for Patients with various forms of cancer are jointly published by the American Cancer Society and the National Comprehensive Cancer Network. Guidelines are available for breast, colon/rectal, lung, prostate, ovarian and skin (melanoma) cancers. Most are available in Spanish and English. One of us recently completed prostate cancer treatment and found the Guidelines on that topic to be the single most useful aid in making the difficult choices required of men with prostate cancer. The guidelines can be obtained from the web sites of either organization, (www.cancer.org) or (www.nccn.org).

American Cancer Society is the comprehensive organization in this field. You can contact them through their web site (www. cancer.org) or by calling 1-800-ACS-2345 anytime. Either a phone call or the web site can help you directly and put you in touch with your local branch of the Society

Diet:

American Dietetics Association (www.eatright.org/) provides advice, materials, and a vast number of links relating to nutrition and diet.

Herman, M. &Ward, E. (1998). *Eat Well & Live Longer: A Sensible Guide & Cookbook for a Healthy Life.* Lincolnwood, IL: Publications International, Ltd. Presented by the editors of *Consumer Guide* and technically reviewed by the American Dietetic Association, this book offers both advice on diet related health issues and appropriate recipes.

Nutrition.gov (www.nutrition.gov) provides links concerning every conceivable nutrition-related issue, including diet and older adults. It is sponsored by a consortium of federal food-related agencies.

Diabetes:

The American Diabetes Association web site provides comprehensive coverage at (www.diabetes. org/main/application/commercewf). Links to research and related organizations are included.

U.S. National Institute of Diabetes & Digestive & Kidney Diseases of the National Institutes of Health (www.niddk.nih.gov/) includes in its web site a vast amount of information on the diseases plus information on research work and funding. Links to relevant reputable sources are included.

American Diabetes Assoc. (editor) (2000). *American Diabetes Association Complete Guide to Diabetes (second edition)*. N.Y.: Bantam Books. Authoritative but easy to read, this inexpensive book provides breadth and depth in self-care for diabetics.

Warshaw, H. & Webb, R. (2001). *The Diabetes Food and Nutrition Bible: A Complete Guide to Planning, Shopping, Cooking, and Eating*. N.Y.: McGraw-Hill. Another work from the American Diabetes Association, this low-cost book covers the arena regarding diet for diabetics, including over 100 recipes.

Exercise:

Fenton, M. (2001). *The Complete Guide to Walking for Health, Weight Loss, and Fitness*. Guilford, CT.: The Lyons Press. Containing everything about the one exercise almost all seniors can do, this book emphasizes the joys of walking and includes a 52-week planned program.

Nelson, M. (2000). *Strong Women Stay Young*. N.Y.: Bantam Doubleday Dell Publishers. A research-based exercise program for women 40-80.

Seniors-Site Sports, Exercise & Fitness web site at (http://seniors-site.com/sports/index.html) contains easily understood data and practices for seniors wanting to maintain or improve their fitness. Also, it is a sub-link of a very useful general site for seniors (http://seniors-site.com) which has practical content relating to nearly every topic in this book. While not particularly profound, this site can be very useful.

Westcott, W. & Baechle, T. (1998). *Strength Training Past 50*. Champaign, IL: Human Kinetics. This book provides a detailed plan for resistance exercise for strengthening older adults. Some attention is also given to other types of exercise and to related nutrition.

Heart Health and Strokes:

American Heart Association and American Stroke Association (www.amhrt.org/presenter.jhtml?identifier=1200000) are affiliated organizations dealing with all aspects of heart health and strokes. The site contains a vast amount of information on these issues plus links to other reliable resources.

Piscatella, J. & Franklin, B. (2003). *Take a Load Off Your Heart: 114 Things You Can Do to Prevent or Reverse Heart Disease*.

N.Y.: Workman Publishing Co. This inexpensive, practical book covers all the typical approaches to preventing and reversing heart problems, giving special emphasis to stress reduction and self-care.

Wiebers, D. (2002). *Stroke-Free for Life: The Complete Guide to Stroke Prevention and Treatment.* N.Y.: HarperResource. This comprehensive yet inexpensive book, written by the director of the Stroke Research Center at the Mayo Clinic, allows you to analyze your own risk of stroke and develop a specific prevention plan for yourself.

Smoking:

The American Lung Association (www.lungusa.org/) web site provides a great deal of information about smoking and smoking cessation as well as about other lung connected diseases. Links to reputable related sites are included.

Fisher, E. (1998). *American Lung Association 7 Steps to a Smoke-Free Life.* Hoboken, NJ: John Wiley & Sons. This self-care approach, which includes worksheets and checklists, helps you analyze your individual situation and develop a smoking cessation plan that will work for you.

Rogers, J. (1994). *You Can Stop Smoking.* N.Y.: Pocket Books. Jacquelyn Rogers founded the SmokEnders® program to help smokers quit. Her month-long cessation plan has helped many who thought they could never stop.

5

Choices Concerning Your Mental Health

Jerene, John's wife, has demonstrated that mind can conquer matter. At age 69, in addition to being very involved with her children and grand-children, she teaches scripture classes each week in two different parishes, co-manages her parish food bank with John, takes care of all the materi-als used in church services in her parish, and, although she no longer counsels addicts and abused people daily as she once did, she spends a huge amount of time helping hurting people of many ages. She loves to note that in one of her scripture classes she is the oldest person while in the other she is the youngest, with "students" ranging to their mid-nine-ties. She does all this despite many physical impediments—serious arthritis, loss of sight in one eye and cataract surgery in the other, 40 years of total thyroid replacement therapy which recently has created negative physical and mental side-effects, and an unidentified autoim-mune syndrome that has at times kept her under medication for a year at a time and has created allergic reactions to many common foods. Proving that what matters is your state of mind, Jerene considers herself in good health.

Good mental health, studies show, significantly reduces the chance of physical illness and injury, makes recovery from physical illness or injury more likely and more rapid, and makes it possible for people to feel and act healthy despite physical illness or disability, as Jerene's experience illustrates. These alone provide sufficient justification for making the choices that assure good mental health; however, the virtues of a healthy mind go far beyond that.

Here we will look at many of the choices about mental health. However, it's important to note that several related questions are dealt with primarily in other chapters: How will you cope with major loss? What about spiritual and religious questions? And, most important, what kind of interpersonal relationships will you have with family, friends and others? In this chapter we will discuss the answers researchers give to these questions:

- Will you practice an optimistic or pessimistic outlook on life?

- Can using your memory and other intellectual functions prevent or delay their decline with aging?

- What kinds of defenses will you use when interpersonal problems arise—as they always do?

- How will you cope with the every day stresses of living?

- To laugh or not to laugh?

- What if you become depressed?

- Where should you focus your attention—on the past, the present or the future?

Will you practice an optimistic or pessimistic outlook on life? There are two issues here. First, does evidence exist that it makes any difference whether you take an optimistic or pessimistic outlook on life? And, secondly, if it does, can a 60-year-old change outlooks? In summary, yes and yes! So, let's look first at studies showing that optimism can help you live a longer, healthier and happier last third of your life. Then we'll examine the choices you can make, if needed, to upgrade your optimism.

While the 1990 classic *Learned Optimism: How to Change Your Mind and Your Life* by Martin Seligman, Ph.D. remains the leading work on this topic, recent studies continue to support his central point: being positive and optimistic about yourself and life makes a huge difference, both in how long you live and how well. For example, as we began writing this section, results of a study published in the *Journal of Personality and Social Psychology* hit the news. According to Reuters, the study led by Becca Levy of Yale University showed that having a positive view of aging added nearly twice as many years to life as did any of the classic physical life extenders such as no smoking, low cholesterol, low blood pressure, exercise, or lack of obesity. Based on data from the Ohio Longitudinal Study of Aging and Retirement, researchers concluded that having positive views on aging added, on average, an amazing 7.6 years to life. Or, looked at the other way, being pessimistic typically shortened life by 7.6 years.

Dr. Seligman suggests four reasons why being more optimistic extends health and life. First, many studies have shown that pessimism and a consequent sense of helplessness suppress the immune system: "The first way in which optimism might affect your health across your lifetime is by preventing helplessness and thereby keeping immune defenses feistier." Secondly, studies show optimists, who are more likely to believe their own actions can make a difference, to be far more likely to take good care of themselves and to correct health problems as they arise. The third cause noted by Seligman arises from the consequences of bad events, which happen more frequently to pessimists. And other studies show that people who frequently experience bad events, such as divorce or unplanned job changes, are more likely to become ill. Finally, pessimists have been shown to be less likely to seek out social support when something bad happens to them. And, as we have seen, failing to develop a loving support system is perhaps the worst mistake persons in their 60s can make.

Studies we looked at under physical health inevitably agree with these findings. In fact, when Perls and Silver name the six lessons learned from their study of centenarians, "Attitude" heads the list. They add, "Centenarians rarely consider their age a limitation—how a person feels about aging is key to his/her ability to thrive." Likewise, Snowdon cites a study done by the Mayo Clinic that followed identified optimists and pessimists over 30 years and found "significantly more optimists were still alive." Similarly, he notes that for the nuns he studied, evidence of an optimistic outlook contributed to longevity.

This brings us to the second element in the question: Can a 60-year-old do anything about it? Several of Seligman's findings support a positive answer. First, his research has shown that your place on the optimist-pessimist scale is mainly learned behavior, not inborn. And he adds, "The good news is that pessimists can learn the skills of optimism and permanently improve the quality of their lives." Second, he has developed tools to help you analyze your status and specific activities that will help you learn to use optimism when it's needed. In his chapter "The Optimistic Life" he describes a simple process that, if followed, can help you gain the benefits of optimism. Many others—several of which are noted in the chapter resources—have provided guidance in developing positive thinking but few, if any, have done the research to prove their effectiveness as Seligman has, so we recommend his book to those choosing to work on this aspect of their lives.

Seligman says that choosing to learn how to use optimism sets people free: "You can choose to use optimism when you judge that less depression, or more achievement, or better health is the issue. But you can also choose not to use it, when you judge that clear sight or owning up is called for. Learning optimism does not erode your sense of values or your judgment." If you feel the need to evaluate your own levels of optimism, you can do so on Seligman's website http://authentichappiness.org/.

Can using your memory and other intellectual functions prevent or delay their decline with aging? Yes, "use it or lose it" applies to mental as well as physical health. Barring serious disease or injury, actively using memory and other intellectual functions has been proven to be the most effective element in preventing and/or slowing decline. And even where serious disease or injury, e.g., Alzheimer's or a stroke, is present, prior and continuous use contributes positively to rehabilitation and slows further decline. If signs of unusual problems with memory or other mental functions occur, they may be symptoms of physical problems, so, in such cases, consult with your family physician as soon as possible.

Earlier we met Judy, a retired English professor keeping relationships active by volunteering at a food bank, enjoying her grandchildren, and keeping in touch with former students. She enjoyed these activities, but after a year or so of retirement she became quite concerned about not using her mind enough. Knowing that her grandmother and an aunt had both suffered from dementia as they aged added urgency to her con-

cern about keeping her mind active and growing. For years she had met regularly with old friends to discuss books they had read, but she strongly felt the need for something new. Her teen-age grandson provided the idea that solved her problem. "Grandma," he said one day, "you really should get yourself a computer. There is some great stuff you can do if you have one, and we can email each other too."

Having had a good secretary during her working years, Judy had consciously avoided learning about computers. She even had no idea how to turn one on. Nonetheless, her grandson's challenge intrigued her. After further thought and a discussion with her husband, who made it clear he wanted nothing to do with computers, she agreed to get a computer if her grandson and oldest granddaughter would agree to help her when she got stuck. They readily agreed, so in her early sixties she entered the computer age. Looking back, she says it was one of the best choices she has made since her retirement.

Having been a "book" person all her life turned out to be a great advantage when it came to learning a new language—"computerese." During the year or so it took her to become proficient, her grandchildren helped her through many a crisis and taught her tricks no book mentioned. On the other hand, by buying and reading several guides she learned a number of things she could teach them in return. While the process included many frustrating moments, overall, she found it refreshing and challenging.

Now in her late sixties, Judy is the family champion when it comes to finding things on the web as well as in the processing of digital photography. Even her husband finally broke down when he learned he could see where every pitch was thrown in every major league baseball game. Now they have gone so far as to set up a wireless network in their home for their two computers. "The most surprising thing to me about computers," Judy says, "is the enormous range of things they encompass. I can view the greatest art, listen to the finest music, read the latest political speeches, buy the best new books, discuss ideas and issues with people from all over the world, and do a thousand other things without leaving my computer. Only time and my imagination limit me."

Let's get one of the myths about aging out of the way before moving on. Contrary to what many people believe, moderate or severe memory and intellectual impairment is not a significant issue for most people during the final third of life. As Perls and Silver put it as a result of their study of centenarians, "Worries about memory are greatly exaggerated." For example, the data in *Older Americans 2000* show only 4.4 percent of those between 65 and 69 have moderate or severe memory impairment, with less than 1 percent seriously impaired. And while the percentage of impairment increases with age, even among those over 85 almost two-thirds remain free of moderate or serious problems and over four-fifths avoid serious impairment.

On the other hand, research continues to show that changes do occur with age in various types of memory and discrete mental abilities. Generally speaking, those aspects of memory and mental abilities that relate to speed of processing or involve multi-tasking—to use computer-related expressions—tend to become less effective with age. However, much of the research in this area is confounded by the "cohort effect," i.e., whether the results apply generally or are applicable only to a certain generation such as those who experienced the nutritional deprivations common during the depression in the 1930s. The best data from research such as The Seattle Longitudinal Study clearly show that on average the better-educated boomers exhibit less loss than did their less-educated parents and grandparents.

Two other findings must be taken into account in determining whether typical age-related changes in memory and intellectual functions are inevitable or matter in every day life. After summarizing in *Adult Life* all the research on age and memory, Stevens-Long and Commons note "that in all of this research there are always those older individuals who do not appear to exhibit any decline in memory function." In other words, such declines are not genetically hard-wired across the human race. Also, several researchers, including Willis and Schaie of the Seattle Longitudinal Studies, have developed training programs that effectively reversed or prevented declines. In his article "The Course of Adult Intellectual Development," K. Warner Schaie concludes: "The results of the cognitive training studies...suggest that observed ability declines in many community-dwelling older people are probably due to disuse and are consequently reversible, at least in part, for many people." In other words, use of your mind not only prevents decline, it can also restore some of what may have been lost through disuse.

What are some of the choices those in their 60s can make to assure effective mental functioning over the last third of life? First and foremost, do not let yourself become a mental couch potato. If you have always had an active intellectual life, maintain it. If you haven't, it's not too late to develop one. As Vaillant states in *Aging Well*, "Successful aging requires continuing to learn new things." He especially emphasizes the importance of being open to learning from the younger generations and points out that "paradoxically, the Study members who learned the most from the next generation had been also the most successful in caring for them." As he concludes,

"Gusto for education in late life is highly correlated with psychological health."

Roy exemplified this when he was learning to use his new computer software and couldn't get it to properly download the pictures his grandson in Wisconsin had sent him. A long distance phone call to his son, a high school computer science teacher, solved the problem in short order. As Roy puts it, "I spent a lot putting my kids through college, so I might as well take advantage of what they know."

None of this implies that everyone must study the classics of literature or develop an appreciation of Sanskrit, although those would work if they appeal to you. The key is regular and expanded use of mental facilities—anything from doing new crossword puzzles to learning Spanish to developing a better recipe for peach cobbler can help. Learning to use the computer for email, web searches and digital photography is surely one of the more useful ways to accomplish this. It's important that your interest in the activity motivate you to continue and expand your mental exercises. Some writers suggest that developing musical skills such as singing harmony, learning to play a guitar or writing your own tunes effectively exercises parts of the brain often left unused. Extra benefit can be gained if any activity becomes creative. Interestingly, several studies, such as the Harvard Longitudinal Studies, show aging women using their creative powers naturally much more often than men, so men may have to pay special attention to developing creative outlets. If you are so inclined, you can also double the benefits by choosing group activities in which to use your mind. Join a book club. Or a bird watching society. Or learn to play the piano.

We provide an example of this. At ages 70, 69, and 59 and not needing additional income, the three of us decided to write this book. We did it not only to help others in their 60s but also to force ourselves into using our creative mental skills. Doing it as a team has both improved the content and provided us with opportunities to share our professional and personal lives.

And to deal with some of the mental changes that do affect most people, a number of approaches can be taken. For example, to deal with any loss in the ability to process several items in memory at once, do what memory experts do. Write things down—in your daily calendar, on your white board, on your to-do list attached to your refrigerator, on post-it notes, etc. Also, many in their 60s and beyond can benefit by concentrating on one task at a time rather than trying to do several at once as they may have done earlier in life. Even when he was younger John never enjoyed doing several things at once, but given his schedule and responsibilities he often did so. In his sixties he realized that things such as paying bills or filing monthly food bank reports can be completed more accurately and quickly by concentrating on one at a time, so he has converted his son's old bedroom into a private office where concentration is possible.

Finally, it's important to take advantage of the life experiences aging brings. In pointing out that the experience and wisdom of older people may more than compensate for lack of reaction speed and such, Stevens-Long and Commons make an important point: "In life, paradox and uncertainty often prevail. Life is more like a horse race than an intelligence test. The winning bet is a matter of calculating possibilities." Fortunately, older people generally excel at calculating possibilities.

What kinds of defenses will you use when interpersonal problems arise—as they always do? How will you cope with the everyday stresses of living? To laugh or not to laugh?

Stress and interpersonal problems are inevitable facts of life. As long as you live you can't totally avoid them; however, you can choose to reduce them and handle them in a healthy way. In all of this you must remember that things that create stress and problems for one person may not for others. Personality type and life style preferences matter here as elsewhere. Take getting into a big argument over some political issue for example. For some people that would create enough stress to ruin two nights sleep. For others it is just what the doctor ordered to relax them. In this area you need to know yourself well.

At least a dozen times in *Aging Well* Vaillant emphasizes that how you handle difficult life situations makes a huge difference in how well you will age. In fact, what he calls "adaptive coping style" or "mature defenses" is one of the seven factors that assure healthy aging—in this case healthy mental aging. He defines it as the "capacity to turn lemons into lemonade and not turn molehills into mountains." Likewise in his "lessons for successful aging" he includes "savor joy and turn lemons into lemonade." In other words enjoy the good things in life and make the best of those bad things that do occur. He includes four strategies or virtues for mature coping: "Doing as one would be done by (*altruism*); artistic creation to resolve conflict and spinning straw into gold (*sublimation*); a stiff upper lip, patience, seeing the bright side (*suppression*); and the ability not to take oneself too seriously (*humor*)."

A recent newspaper article illustrates the importance of using mature coping skills. The article reported on a huge increase in alcohol and drug abuse among those 60 and above. In it Joe Lang told how he became depressed when forced to retire. Instead of finding some other way to make his life meaningful, he drank nearly two fifths of booze each day for almost two years. Fortunately, he finally realized how he was wasting his life and sought help. Today he builds houses for Habitat for Humanity as a volunteer, and serves as his precinct's committeeman. He enjoys life once again.

As Perls and Silver point out in *Living to 100*, "Longevity is not a result of having avoided stress, but rather of having responded to it efficiently and effectively." They had given the NEO Five-Factor Inventory of personality to their centenarians and found them to be much like the general population except that they were significantly *lower* in "neuroticism," which measures "unhealthy feelings, like anger, fear, guilt, and sadness." Summarizing, they say, "Coping with stress, or quickly getting over life's emotional setbacks, is therefore one of the most important factors in successful aging." Elsewhere they add, "Determination and energy to overcome obstacles appear to be more important to longevity than traveling the easy road in life."

Some of the choices you can make to deal with problems and reduce stress are obvious from earlier sections—exercise, for example, or entering a stress reduction program at a nearby community center. Many approaches adapted from religious traditions, such as yoga, meditation, or retreats, may help you. In addition, you can work at developing the kinds of mature defenses that Valliant and others have shown lead to resilience. Speaking of the strengths you should have as you pass through your 60s, Sheehy says, "Resilience is probably the most important protection you can have."

There are two other major ways to deal with life's problems and stress: positive relationships with family and friends, which we discussed in depth in an earlier chapter, and developing a good sense of humor. The latter is one of the few elements of healthy aging that every study seems to agree upon. Laughing is just flat out good for you, so be sure to build it into your life. In *Living to 100* the authors say, "A visible and consistent component of the centenarian repertoire is humor." After listing "Retain sense of humor" as one of the six ways to "grow old with grace," Vaillant elicits a chuckle when he summarizes the point thus: "Long, happy marriages have a lot in common with successful aging. They are hard work. Both require a healthy dose of tolerance, commitment, maturity, and a sense of humor."

What if you become depressed? All of us become depressed at times. The critical issues are, "What sort of depression is it?" and "What can you choose to do about it?"

If your favorite team loses the World Series, you may go to bed depressed, even thinking nothing good can ever happen again. But if the next morning you devour a good breakfast and find yourself cracking slightly off-color jokes at your spouse, there's no sense in worrying about your passing depression.

At the other extreme, if you realize your moods persistently swing wildly between deep depression and manic liveliness, you probably have a physical disease—bipolar or manic-depression. Modern drug therapy can control almost all bipolar depression, which typically has a genetic physical cause. Seek medical help immediately!

More difficult to diagnose and determine effective treatment for is a third type of depression—variously labeled unipolar or clinical or "normal" depression. Causes of this sort of depression can include thyroid deficiency, alcoholism, some medications, illness, personal tragedy, or in a minority of cases a genetic flaw. And it can range from quite mild and temporary to very severe and permanent unless treated.

In *Learned Optimism* Seligman indicates that his studies have shown that at any given moment about 25 percent of us are at least mildly depressed. Other studies show that the rate of severe depression grows slightly with age. About 16 percent are *severely* depressed in the 65 to 69 age group and 23 percent among those over 85, according to *Older Americans 2000*. Also, Liz Taylor, who writes the "Growing Older" column for *The Seattle Times*, says, "Adults older than 65 constitute 13 percent of the U.S. population, yet account for 19 percent of suicides." Taylor believes undiagnosed and untreated depression accounts for most of this anomaly. Vaillant supports this by pointing out that for the subjects of the Harvard Longitudinal Study the two things that most commonly destroyed or reversed healthy maturation were alcoholism and major depression. He calls them "organic insults to the brain." Clearly, then, preventing severe depression and identifying and seeking treatment for it when present are critical choice issues for those wanting to maintain good health in their 60s and beyond.

Since clinical depression can almost always be treated effectively with cognitive therapy and/or drugs, knowing its symptoms is essential. To quote advertisements frequently run by the National Mental Health Association: "If the symptoms on this list sound familiar, tell a doctor. Because if you have several of these symptoms for two weeks or more, you could have clinical depression." The list includes these ten symptoms:

- "Feelings of sadness or irritability,

- Loss of interest or pleasure in activities once enjoyed,

- Changes in weight or appetite,

- Changes in sleep pattern,

- Feeling guilty, hopeless or worthless,

- Inability to concentrate, remember things, or make decisions,

- Fatigue or loss of energy,

- Restlessness or decreased activity,

- Complaints of physical aches and pains for which no medical explanation can be found, and

- Thoughts of death or suicide."

Note three things about the list of symptoms. First, everyone has exhibited most of these symptoms at some time or other. Second, for several of the symptoms it's the divergence from normal that matters, not the specific change. For example, with weight and appetite it is symptomatic whether you gain or loose, eat more or less. Third, it takes having several of these symptoms—some say five or more—over at least a couple weeks to indicate a severe depression unlikely to vanish on its own.

Obviously, good mental health requires treatment of severe depression, but less obviously, so does good physical health. Studies have proven that depression suppresses the immune system, which both leads to illness and slows recuperation. Depression also is a risk factor for both heart disease and strokes. And as Snowdon points out in *Aging with Grace*, even small strokes increase the risk of dementia from Alzheimer's disease.

Depression is not something to delay getting treatment for. Unfortunately, according to Liz Taylor, 70 percent of older adults who committed suicide had visited a physician within a month of death and 20 percent had been there the day of suicide. So, if you go for help, don't rely on your physician or therapist to discover your problem. You need to be very specific about laying out the symptoms you have been experiencing and asking for treatment.

When Paul's wife died after a long, happy marriage, his family and friends worried the he would be devastated by his loss. With their help, he kept very busy and held up well for nearly a year. Then he began having a series of illnesses. He was clearly depressed, but he kept up a good front, and his physician only treated the physical problems, one at a time. Finally, one of Paul's sons confronted him and told him that he needed therapy. It was not easy for Paul to admit this, but when he did, the therapist led him to some new strategies that enabled him to recover his natural optimism.

Such medical treatment with drugs and/or cognitive therapy should surely be used if you or a loved one currently suffers from depression. However, given the losses normal life inflicts on those 60 and beyond, it is just as important to build defenses against severe depression before it strikes. The most important defense is learning how to use optimism and positive thinking to avoid feelings of helplessness—as discussed above. And where side effects of medications or alcohol abuse may be the causal factors, those must be dealt with directly. Finally, supporting family, helpers, and friends can make a huge difference, as was discussed earlier in the chapter on relationships.

Where should you focus your attention—on the past, the present or the future? At first glance this seems an odd question to address in relation to mental health in the 60s and beyond, but given the consistency of what researchers are finding on this topic, it is worth a brief look.

As people pass from youth through middle age and on to old age, the way they think about time usually changes. Up to about 50 most see the future as better than either the present or past, according to research reported upon in *Adult Life*. From around 50 through their late 60s most see the past, present and future "as about equally negative or positive." After that the past is generally seen as better than the present and the future as worse than the present. However, the authors continue, "There are also data to support the notion that the most competent older people are those who are *not* heavily invested in the future. They may plan for the future, but they do not live in it. Neither do they dwell in the past, although they have learned to consider the past as well as the present and future."

Studies of even older adults support those findings. For example, Sheehy reports on a longitudinal study by Cecelia Hurwich of women in their 70s through 90s who "had remained active and creative." Hurwich says, "They live very much in the present but they always have plans for the future." Likewise, in their study of centenarians Perls and Silver found them "ready for death but still engaged in life. They no longer think about past mistakes or losses, nor do they struggle to integrate the contradictions and ambivalences of their long lives. They don't ruminate about whether or not their lives had meaning—they are still actively involved in finding meaning in their lives."

One of the things that differentiated those aging successfully from others in the Harvard study was the ability by late middle age to forgive injuries in the past and get on with the present. They were also able to "spend time in the past and take sustenance from past accomplishments" while in the present learning from the next generation. And, again, while they had goals for the future, Vaillant says those aging successfully "seize the day, but only one day at a time."

The experience of our friend Angela illustrates the importance of letting the past go. Angela's daughter Jennifer left home at 18 after one final blow-out with her mother over Angela's new husband. During the next 20 years, Jennifer moved away, married and had two daughters of her own, but she had no contact with her mother. When Angela learned that Jennifer's high school class was holding their 20-year reunion, she got Jennifer's address from the reunion committee and wrote a note apologizing for her part in their quarrel and asking to see Jennifer and her daughters. The resulting reconciliation gave Angela the gratification of being a grandparent—for the cost of a postage stamp and some pride.

Since this focus on "today" that characterizes effective aging is very similar to that taught in many self-help groups, you can easily find assistance in developing it in your own life should you choose to do so.

In subsequent chapters we will look at several other topics that can affect health such as financial matters, insurance issues, and building meaning into your life, including religious and spiritual issues.

RESOURCES

Almost all the general book and web site resources found in the previous chapter on physical health are relevant here as well. For example the National Institute of Health web site MEDLINEplus contains sections and links on depression, including bipolar disorder, memory, dementia, stress, and suicide as well a general section on mental health, per se. Following are a few books and web sites dealing generally with mental health issues.

Books:

In the area of mental health for seniors, general books typically are oriented toward professionals such as psychologists or counselors. Therefore only a couple of examples will be listed here.

Butler, R., et al. (1998). *Aging and Mental Health: Positive Psychosocial and Biomedical Approaches (5th edition)*. Boston: Allyn & Bacon

Qualls, S. (1998). *Aging and Mental Health (Understanding Aging)*. Malden, MA: Blackwell Publishers.

Web Sites:

The Center for Mental Health Services (www.mentalhealth.org/default.asp) is a service of the Substance Abuse and Mental Health Services Administration of the Dept. of Health and Human Services. It provides information on many mental health issues as well as links to related sites.

Internet Mental Health (www.mentalhealth.com/p.html), a service provided by a Canadian psychiatrist, provides a comprehensive set of links on mental health issues as well as discussions of most specific mental health problems. It takes an international perspective.

National Institute of Mental Health (www.nimh.nih.gov), a unit of the federal National Institute of Health, provides information on mental health issues with special emphasis on research. Links to related sites are included.

National Mental Health Association (www.nmha.org/), the largest nonprofit involved in mental health, provides information, publications, links, and locations of local affiliates.

Below are written material and web sites relating to the specific topics discussed in the chapter. Because all of these topics are also covered in the general books and web sites listed above and in the previous chapter, only a few key resources are included here.

Depression:

Ludman, E., Simon, G. & Katon, W. (2002). *The Depression Handbook*. Seattle: Bull Publishing. Although solidly based on research, this inexpensive book provides practical self-care help for those dealing with depression.

Wright, J. & Basco, M. (2001). *Getting Your Life Back: The Complete Guide to Recovery from Depression*. N.Y.: Free Press. Inexpensive and written in plain language, this book provides insight and self-care for sufferers with minor or clinical depression.

The Depression and Bipolar Support Alliance (www.ndmda.org/index.html) is a nonprofit organization that provides information and support to those with depression and other mood disorders. A comprehensive list is provided of links to related web sites and to information on how to contact affiliated local support groups.

Humor and Mental Health:

Association for Applied and Therapeutic Humor (www.aath.org/) proves there is an association for every possible topic. In addition it includes a great bibliography of works on the topic of humor and many aspects of health.

Bates, R. et al. (1995). *How to Be Funnier: Happier, Healthier, and More Successful Too.* Minneapolis: Trafton Publishers. Funny and easy to read, this book can help anyone improve her or his sense of humor and presentation skills using humor.

Klein, A. (1989). *The Healing Power of Humor: Techniques for Getting Through Loss, Setbacks, Upsets, Disappointments, Difficulties, Trials, Tribulations, and All That.* N.Y.: J.P. Tarcher. This simple, inexpensive book has been through over 24 printings proving that it lives up to its title.

Meyer, K. (1994). *How to Shit in the Woods: An Environmentally Sound Approach to a Lost Art.* Berkeley, CA: Ten Speed Press. We put this in just to see if you are reading carefully and still have a sense of humor. We swear it is a real book—on how to keep the forest clean.

Memory and Intellectual Skills:

McKhann, G. & Albert, M. (2002). *Keep Your Brain Young: The Complete Guide to Physical and Emotional Health and Longevity.* Hoboken, NJ: John Wiley & Sons. This easy to read and inexpensive book covers ways to keep memory and intellect functioning well while aging plus many other aspects of the aging brain.

Resource Center on Aging Univ. of California Berkeley (http://ist-socrates.berkeley.edu/~aging/index.html) has information and a huge number of web links to many topics relating to aging, including memory and intellectual issues.

Small, G. (2002). *The Memory Bible: An Innovative Strategy for Keeping Your Brain Young.* N.Y.: Hyperion. Written by the Director of the UCLA Memory and Aging Research Center (www.memory.ucla.edu/), this book prescribes tips for keeping your brain fit and delaying or preventing dementia.

Victoroff, J. (2002). *Saving Your Brain: The Revolutionary Plan to Boost Brain Power, Improve Memory, and Protect Yourself Against Aging and Alzheimer's.* N.Y.: Bantam, Doubleday Dell Publishers. Director of Neurobehavior at the Rancho Los Amigos National Rehabilitation Center (www.rancho.org) the author provides a well-written summary of research on these topics as well as prescribing specific steps for maintaining mental fitness.

Optimism/Positive Thinking:

Authentic Happiness web site (http://authentichappiness.org/) relates not only to our later chapters but to mental health as well. Martin Seligman, the author of *Learned Optimism,* and colleagues provide and score for you many questionnaires related to the topic, including an optimism/pessimism scale.

Luciani, J. (2001). *Self-Coaching: How to Heal Anxiety and Depression.* Hoboken, NJ: John Wiley & Sons. Although primarily oriented toward ending anxiety or depression, the methodology is essentially reorienting self-talk toward positive thoughts.

Snyder, C. (1994). *Psychology of Hope: You Can Get There from Here.* N.Y.: Free Press. This analysis of the importance of hope in life includes self-analysis tools and specific action plans for becoming more hopeful.

Stress:

Davis, M. et al. (2000). *The Relaxation & Stress Reduction Workbook (5th edition).* Oakland, CA: New Harbinger Publishing. Truly a workbook, this work contains many self-assessment tools and a great variety of stress management approaches.

Kabat-Zinn, J. (1990). *Full Catastrophe Living: Using the Wisdom of Your Body and Mind to Face Stress, Pain, and Illness.* N.Y.:Delacorte. The founder of the University of Massachusetts Medical Center clinic for stress reduction explains how practices such as meditation and yoga have been proven effective in dealing with stress, pain and illness. A specific plan is included. It is available in six languages.

The International Stress Management Association UK (www.isma.org.uk/index.htm) provides an international perspective on stress issues. Excellent links are provided including one to the U.S. affiliate (www.isma-usa.org/) which provides similar information from an American perspective.

Seaward, B. (2002). *Managing Stress: Principles and Strategies for Health and Well-Being (3rd edition)*. Boston: Jones & Bartlett Publishing. A large book that comprehensively covers the topic, it includes the research base and specific proven stress management techniques. Some consider this *the* text in this field.

6

Finances and Your Sixties Transition

"I never thought I would be this well off when I got older," Larry commented when the discussion turned to questions of finance. "But, of course, these last couple of years have been different and I don't know where we will end up with our investments. Besides Social Security, I have been paying into my 403 (b) pension plan through my job at the college, and my employer has been matching my contribution. But I guess I was greedy. I invested my pension funds in high growth tech funds during the late 90's. For a while there was great growth, but then some of my funds dropped in value up to ninety percent. My biggest holding was worth $45 per share in 2000 and dropped to $5. Today it is worth $19 and is coming back slowly from the bottom, but I don't know where I will be in the next ten to twenty years. I'd been counting on that money to continue to grow like it did in the 90's."

This captures the dilemma facing many people in the early years of the twenty-first century. Pensions and investments increased dramatically through the 1990's, allowing people to contemplate major changes in their lifestyles, only to have their dreams come crashing down in 2000-2002. While the picture became somewhat brighter later, what the financial future will hold is always unclear. And so planning for finances during the sixties transition must take this uncertainty into account.

As we've seen, a major decision of the sixties is when to retire. And while other factors from pleasure in the job to desire for freedom influence that decision, certainly one major factor is your financial situation. Can you afford to retire? This chapter will explore some of the basic facts of financial planning and will conclude with a summary of resources for making financial decisions.

There are some general rules of thumb concerning finances for you to consider as you contemplate a change in employment. If you want to maintain your established lifestyle, one recommendation is that you should be able to project an annual income between 60 and 85 percent of past income. This income may come from Social Security, pensions, retirement accounts such as 401(k)s, 403(b)s, and IRAs, and personal savings. Several assumptions are implicit in giving this needed-income rule of thumb. First, it assumes that there are no longer any mortgage payments on your house. You should have fewer work expenses, such as commuting, professional dress, and meals out. But retirement brings other expenses. With free time, you may shop more, eat out more, and travel extensively. You must make a careful analysis of the reality of future financial needs and opportunities.

What will Social Security provide for you? Larry had been contributing to Social Security since he began working in his late teens. His top salary was about $50,000. If he does decide to retire and start collecting Social Security when he is 62, his monthly payments will be about $1000. Larry is realizing that this won't support him and his wife in anything like the lifestyle they have had. Can Larry retire?

For many, Social Security is the foundation of financial planning. But there are some rules for understanding just what you can expect from this source. For example, in 2005 to be eligible for Social Security, you had to have worked in a program that contributes to Social Security for a minimum of ten years and you had to have earned a minimum of forty work credits. Note that many jobs do not pay in to Social Security, so you may not qualify. Some who work for government agencies or religious groups and self-employed people who haven't paid in to Social Security may not be eligible. You can check regularly with the Social Security Administration to get an estimate of what you can anticipate when you start to draw benefits. And an annual statement of benefits is mailed to each person in the Social Security program. This can give you an idea of what to expect when you retire. At least six months before you wish to access the system, you should carefully research what is available and what you are eligible for, and begin the process of application. The Social Security Administration maintains an excellent website with answers to many questions about benefits of the program.

Delight's friend Helen is faced with problems about Social Security and Medicare eligibility. Twenty years ago she and her husband moved to Illinois where he had obtained a teaching position at a state university. She quickly got a job teaching in a local public high school nearby. But it turns out that state employees in Illinois do not pay in to Social Security; consequently neither Helen nor her husband is eligible for payments at retirement nor are they eligible for Medicare. She has learned from the Social Security Administration that she earned 36 of the 40 quarterly credits required for eligibility. She earned them in various positions she held during and after college and before her move to Illinois. Now retiring from her Illinois teaching position, she can become eligible for Social Security and Medicare benefits if she works only four more quarters. Helen is currently exploring positions in book stores or perhaps a local library to work for a year to earn the necessary credits. She must be sure only to accept a job that contributes to Social Security.

You can begin receiving Social Security payments after age 62, but the longer you wait, the bigger the ultimate monthly payment will be. The year you were born determines when you are eligible for full payments. For example, if you started to collect at age 62 rather than waiting and you were born before 1938 you would have received 20 percent smaller payments for the rest of your life. If you were born between 1943 and 1954, however, your payments would be 25 percent less. At 63 and born before 1938 the payments would have been reduced by 13.5 percent, and at 64 the payments would have been 6.66 percent lower than full payments.

One recent change makes it more attractive to continue working past age 65. Until 2000, people between the ages of 65 and 70 had their Social Security benefits reduced by one dollar for every three they earned over $17,000 a year. A tax law that President Clinton signed in May 2000 allows workers over 65 to earn any amount of money and still draw the full Social Security payments for which they are eligible. An excellent article published in the August, 2002 *Consumer Reports* summarizes some of the issues and choices in deciding to work past age 65.

The following chart shows at what age people born between 1938 and 1954 can begin receiving full benefits.

Year of Birth	When you will receive full payments
1937 or earlier	Age 65
1938	Age 65 and two months
1939	Age 65 and four months
1940	Age 65 and six months
1941	Age 65 and eight months
1942	Age 65 and ten months
1943-1954	Age 66

For people born after 1954, the table again climbs by two-month increments, and people born in 1960 and later will not receive full benefits until age 67.

At first glance, it may seem attractive to start receiving payments at age 62, but in fact with the much longer life expectancy, from a purely financial standpoint it may be smarter to wait to collect Social Security until you are eligible for full benefits, or even wait longer if you will accrue more credits which will push your final payments higher. On the other hand, some believe that you are better off taking the lesser amount of money starting when you are 62, either because it does in fact allow you to retire at that time, or because you may be able to invest it more efficiently than by leaving it with the government. As you plan to claim Social Security payments, you should calculate the options very carefully and make the best decision for your circumstances. This is one place you may not easily change your mind after the decision has been made.

Jim decided to retire at age 62. He drew Social Security and had some other sources of income. But he had always enjoyed his work. His job as a technician had been both demanding and exciting. Within months he was bored with his life. He decided to go back to work. He found that he could stop drawing his Social Security and later reinstate the program, so that the money he earned would raise the final payments he would receive at the time he did retire again.

Here are some specific examples of estimated benefits figured on an annual salary of $50,000 and kept in constant 2004 dollars.

Age 40 in 2004	Age 50 in 2004	Age 60 in 2004
Age 62 in 2026 Monthly payment $1103	Age 62 in 2016 Monthly payment $1111	Age 62 in 2006 Monthly payment $979
Age 67 in 2031 Monthly payment $1588	Age 66 in 2020 Monthly payment $1531	Age 66 in 2010 Monthly payment $1373
Age 70 in 2034 Monthly payment $1981	Age 70 in 2024 Monthly payment $2055	Age 70 in 2014 Monthly payment $1903

These figures are taken from Social Security Quick Calculator on the Social Security Administration web site. To learn about your own personal possible payments, you should contact the Social Security Administration. You can request a statement that shows your potential payment, based on continued employment similar to current employment. You'll find contact information in the resources for this chapter.

Spousal payments through Social Security are another thing to consider. According to the Social Security literature, if you're receiving retirement benefits, your wife or husband may also receive benefits at age 62 or before that if he or she is taking care of your child who is under age 16 or disabled. Your spouse receives about one half of your full-retirement age benefit unless she or he begins collecting benefits before full-retirement age. In that case, the amount of the spouse's benefit is permanently reduced by a percentage based on the number of months before she or he reaches full-retirement age. When an individual is eligible both for retirement benefits on his or her own Social Security record and for benefits as a spouse, Social Security always pays the higher amount.

If there is more than one dependant—a spouse and child or two or more children—the benefits paid are combined and are called family benefits. The maximum family benefit is 150% to 180% of the retired worker's benefits. A Social Security formula figures out the exact amount for which a family is eligible. If there is a wife and a child, the family benefit might be 180% of the individual's benefit, but when the child reaches 18, unless that child is disabled, the benefit would drop to 150% of the worker's benefits. This represents 100% for the worker and 50% for the spouse.

If the individual receiving benefits dies, survivors benefits, which is how these benefits are referred to in the Social Security web site, can be paid to certain family members, including the beneficiary's widow or widower, dependent children and dependent parents. An excellent booklet contains more information about filing for these benefits and can be downloaded from the Social Security site under Survivors by clicking on the title *Survivors Benefits* (Publication No.05-10084). The main thing to understand when considering Social Security provisions is to be clear about what benefits each of the couple will receive, and what will happen to the remaining spouse at the death of the first spouse.

Delight retired before she turned 62, but her husband died just as she was reaching that age. As an unemployed widow, she then became eligible to receive most of her husband's Social Security payments. If she elected to draw benefits from her own account when she reached 62, she would lose that survivors benefit. The two benefit amounts were very similar. So she chose to continue to receive her husband's benefit and wait until she was 66 or perhaps 70 before drawing her own account. At either of those points the amount she would receive from her own account would be much higher.

But during her counseling appointment with Social Security, a second point relevant to this issue was raised. Delight had been approached to go back to teaching part time at Seattle University. However, if she earned over a certain amount, she would no longer be eligible for survivors benefits. Because the salary she would earn and the benefit she was receiving were almost the same, she decided not to work and pay for commuting, clothes, meals, and other expenses. The advisor did tell her that this rule will probably be different in 2006.

Because the rules are constantly changing, always take the time to get current advice from professionals in the field. Delight was able to make the best decisions for herself because she met with a good Social Security counselor to learn all of her options and to make sure she understood the results of possible decisions.

What about other pensions? Many non-profit organizations, companies, and governmental agencies have pension programs that provide retirement income. Talk to your human resource office or union representative to learn exactly what is available to you.

A key tip is to see if there are pension benefits owed on positions held many years ago. For example, a person who worked as a school-teacher from age 25 to 37 may well be owed pension benefits when turning 59 1/2 or 65, depending on the policy. If you track your career history backward you may find a pension you didn't realize you were eligible for.

Karl's experience provides a great example of this. He served as a registrar and development director for many years at a university and com-

munity college in a state that, like many, has two plans for retiring faculty—an older one providing an excellent retirement income and a newer, much less generous one. At the point Karl wished to retire for health reasons, he fell one year short of qualifying for the better plan. While carefully reviewing his career with the personnel office, he discovered that the state system applied all government work in determining eligibility. Since he had worked for the post office for two years while in college 45 years before, he became eligible for a much greater retirement income.

There has been a trend in recent years at some companies to avoid pensions in favor of other investment plans. Increasingly, organizations may use other types of retirement programs such as 401(k) or 403(b) programs. Often in these situations the employee selects a fund and has some salary placed in that account. Many companies will match some or the entire amount the employee places in this account. Funds are tax deferred, so that you pay at the time you begin to withdraw money. This is usually at age 59 1/2 or later, but not later than age 70. This means that you control the investments, at least to some extent. In the stock market of the 1990's, many people did very well with 401(k) plans. But later many saw their 401(k) funds diminish rapidly. One of the main causes was poor diversity in allocation of the money in the fund. Some employers caused this by insisting that 401(k) funds be kept in company stock. When those stock prices declined sharply, and because individuals were not allowed to sell out, billions of potential retirement dollars were lost. Events such as that should serve as a wakeup call to all. Careful financial planning for retirement, including diversification of your investments, is critical to your financial well-being in the last decades of your life.

Should you manage your own investments? Social Security and pension funds are generally managed for you. If these are your only sources of income in retirement, managing investments is irrelevant. But the trend in many retirement plans has been to provide more responsibility as well as authority for managing your own retirement resources. And possible changes in the Social Security also may provide more individual authority over a portion of Social Security retirement funds. For this reason it is increasingly important to develop some basic understanding of money management.

Many financial planners say that the first step is to eliminate debt. Do not get a new mortgage on your house—pay off the old one. Do not carry credit card debt. These debts can cost you 15-20 percent per year in interest. Keep your old car instead of buying, or worse, leasing a new car. Analyze your current debts realistically and then move to pay them off. This can be a major challenge for individuals who have lived too long by moving from one credit card to another, building up a balance in each and paying the minimum from another credit card. This dangerous practice can bring on financial ruin. If you are in this situation, there are agencies that may be able to help you to consolidate your debts and develop a realistic payment plan. If you work with one, tear up your credit cards, and live only on cash, your lifestyle may go down, but you will be working for a more secure future.

As you begin to move toward retirement, and once your debts are paid off, you should continue to take at least the same amount of money that you used for your debts and place it in your "retirement" account. This money should be set aside for the long haul. You should establish one or more accounts to which you deposit funds regularly. This account should be set up to grow but also to be fairly stable.

Delight has always been interested in investing, and looking forward to her new time in retirement she has begun to pay more attention to the stock market. But she was given good advice: Take a small amount, like 10 percent of the retirement funds available, and put that in a trading account. She was told to use that account to "play with" and see if she could really make money. But she was advised to leave the rest in a conservative account that will grow and provide ongoing income. So far, the investments she has made following advice from an investment advisory service have outperformed the conservative account.

Many financial experts recommend placing money in mutual funds, but you must be careful about several factors in choosing mutual funds. First, most charge a management fee. It is often 1 to 1.5 percent or more. In times of very low interest rates, this management fee can take away almost all growth in your fund. So check the management fee carefully. No-load funds often have very low fees, especially if the money is left to accumulate for a number of years. Some advisors say that Vanguard Funds are especially attractive, but be sure to verify current fees. To get a listing of funds, go to the Morningstar site included in the chapter resources. This is a complicated web site, but it has valuable free information on investing.

Again, a key rule for effective investing is called asset allocation. The important rule here is to have parts of your investment savings in a number of different investment categories. This means, for example, that you will not put all your money into technology stocks. Too many people think owning several different stocks in the same category means they have good asset allocation. But in fact, the stocks within categories usually move together, both up and down! Instead, to have good asset allocation, you want to have some money in consumer stocks, some in energy stocks, some in financial stocks, etc. You want to have some money in stocks or stock funds, some money in bonds, and some money in readily accessible sources like bank accounts or Certificates of Deposit. When you are younger you should have more money in stocks, which over the long run are likely to grow the most, but as you get closer to retirement, you should change your investments to more conservative funds that are less likely to swing downward strongly. One rule of thumb is to subtract your age from 100. What is left is the percentage you should have in stocks.

At age 62, Mary recognized that she would soon retire from her public school teaching job and would need to plan carefully for her own financial future. She reviewed the money she had saved toward retirement, then put 38 percent of her funds into stocks and 62 percent into bonds, treasury bills and other money sources. She plans to rebalance her account carefully each year as she gets older to keep a good distribution between stocks and other "money funds."

Using a different approach, another investment advisory group makes two general recommendations. In 2004 they recommended asset allocation of 30 percent in US stocks, 30 percent in international stocks, 10 percent in inflation-adjusted treasury bills, 10 percent in high yield corporate bonds, 10 percent in high grade corporate bonds, 5 percent in Real Estate Investment Trusts (REIT's) and 5 percent in precious metals. Secondly, they suggested that you have no more than 4 percent of your assets in any one single stock. While this recommendation is not specifically for people who are moving toward retirement, a formula such as this shows how important it is to hold a diverse set of investments.

Depending on your retirement plan, you may have more flexibility than you think. The organization from which Delight retired puts a sum equal to 10 percent of the annual salary into a 403(b) plan. She could match up to 10 percent and she had the right to choose between two investment agencies—TIAA-CREF or Fidelity. Each of these organizations has many funds to choose among. So Delight could choose to put some of her retirement plan money in a high-growth fund, some into a foreign stocks fund, more into a bond fund, and perhaps some into an inflation-protected bond fund. The decision was hers, within the offerings of the fund family. It was these decisions that allowed her to get the diversity discussed above that is so important to financial health. Generally several switches among funds are permitted each year without fee.

Social Security is the safety net to most in our society today. It provides basic support as well as medical care for those who are seriously ill and for those who are disabled. For those who have worked enough to qualify, it provides some income. But that amount is very limited. People must realize that Social Security alone at age 65 will not provide for a prosperous lifestyle.

Is your house your biggest asset? *Delight's close friend Bonnie, age 62, has dealt with this situation. Bonnie's mother is now 84. Widowed once at age 50, she married again, but was widowed a second time when she was 65. She had some limited investments, received some life insurance, and got the widow's benefit from Social Security, but as a housewife and mother, she had never earned any Social Security credits of her own. By living very frugally, she managed to continue for almost* *twenty years. But then the money ran out. When her children got involved in reviewing her options with her, it became painfully apparent that her only choice was to sell the house she had grown up in, and, with her husband, purchased from her parents 45 years earlier. Her children had grown up in this house. She owned the house without a mortgage, and its value had gone up a lot in that 45 years. But she loved it; it was really the only home she had ever known. The sad decision was made, and the house was put on the market. It sold more rapidly than expected and she had to find a place to purchase and move to, all within a matter of weeks. But, from the sale of the house she can pay the taxes and purchase a new, modest cottage, and put the rest of the purchase price into bonds. Her children think that if she continues with her frugal lifestyle, she will be able to live another twenty years on the money she has gotten from the sale of her home.*

Often your home is your biggest asset. With the increase in real estate values over recent decades, you may have a major source of funds within your home. But you must decide what to do with these funds. Do you want to stay in this house for the foreseeable future? Is the house fully paid for? Are the property taxes reasonable?

If you choose to stay in your current home, but need additional income, one possibility is a reverse mortgage. This allows home owners over the age of 62 to draw down equity in their homes while still living in them. A reverse mortgage is a loan against your home that you do not have to pay back for as long as you live there. It can be paid to you all at once, as a regular monthly advance, or at times and in amounts that you choose. You pay the money back plus interest when you die, sell your home, or permanently move out of your home. This doesn't contradict the advice to pay off your mortgage, in that a reverse mortgage gives you money and you don't have to make payments every month. The down side of this opportunity is that it removes the home from your estate. For more on reverse mortgages, see the reference section.

Would you be more satisfied if the resources currently tied up in your home are invested in income-producing investments? If so, you need to consider where and how you would live. Does moving to a smaller house, apartment or condominium appeal to you? There also are a wide variety of opportunities in senior "adult" community retirement living. These range from complexes offering totally independent living for people above a certain age, say 55, to assisted living, to nursing homes. The best options for many people are special facilities that have a variety of living arrangements.

A good choice for Delight's distant relative, Betsy, has been a high-rise facility called The Sequoias in downtown San Francisco. There you can buy a studio, one-bedroom, or two-bedroom apartment. All meals are provided. Guest rooms are available for short-term rental so Betsy can easily entertain members of her family for several-day visits. Recreational, library, hair care, and other services are located in the building. Morning door checks assure that no problems have arisen during the night. But should a resident need to have assisted care provided in the apartment, it is available. Should the person need to move into the nursing floor, it is in the same facility. This allows couples to stay near each other if one requires full care. For example, about a year ago, Betsy had failed to the point where the nursing staff informed her family that she really needed the continuous care provided in the nursing wing. She was becoming confused and might fall and not be found for hours. The difficult decision was made to move her from her 24th floor apartment where she had lived happily for over twenty years to a single room in the 2nd floor nursing wing. But the people were the same. The facility was very supportive. Friends could continue to visit. And, while very sad, this has proven to be a good solution for a single woman in her eighties.

If a person is in the nursing wing for a prolonged period, and it is clear that the original apartment will never be used again, it reverts to the association and the association can resell it. When a resident dies, the apartment reverts to the organization. In this arrangement, an individual or couple buys into the complex for one initial purchase price and then pays a monthly fee that includes all care, services and meals. But because it reverts to the association on the death of the resident the value of the apartment is not part of the individual's estate. There are similar sites in most cities.

When you make the decision about whether and when to retire, finances are a major consideration. Can you afford to retire and live a comfortable lifestyle into the future? You must do careful financial planning, be realistic about how much you will really spend each year, and investigate the many alternative living arrangements available to all of us in the last third of our lives. And the many options and choices are exciting!

RESOURCES

Many excellent books and web sites deal with matters of retirement planning, Social Security, pensions, and other financial matters. Listed below are some of the relatively recent books and web sites that deal with the topics of this chapter.

Books:

Hinden, J. (2001). *How to Retire Happy: Everything you Need to Know About the 12 Most Important Decisions You Must Make Before You Retire*. New York: McGraw-Hill. This very readable book deals with many of the key issues that must be faced in planning for retirement. It contains a lot of useful advice about the personal, economic, and practical problems that one will face when deciding to retire.

Matthews, J. with Berman, D. (2002). *Social Security, Medicare & Government Pensions (8th edition)*. Berkeley: Nolo. Filled with specific information about how to apply for Social Security, who is eligible and when one may be eligible information on Medicare, and on government pensions, this excellent, easily-read book is a valuable resource for anyone who wants to learn about possible benefits for which one is eligible.

U.S. Dept. of Health and Human Services. (2005). *Medicare and You 2006*. Publication No. CMS-10050. This free annual handbook provides a great deal of information about what services are available through Medicare and how Medicare may work in conjunction with other medical plans.

Wasik, J. (1999). *Retire Early—And Live the Life You Want Now*. New York: Henry Holt. Intended for decision-making prior to actually retiring, this book provides good insights into financial planning and other decisions that should be made before the actual step of retirement is taken.

Wolman, W. & Colamosca, A. (2002). *The Great 401 (k) H()ax [sic]*. Cambridge: Perseus Publishing. Unlike other books that suggest the ease with which one can move financially into retirement, this book raises serious issues about the risks the authors contend are associated with the false sense of security about the stock market that is the backbone for 401(k) programs. It provides an interesting alternative perspective for retirement planning.

Web Sites: What follows are merely a few of the many websites that provide current information about financial planning.

AARP (formerly the American Associate of Retired Persons) (www.AARP.org) provides excellent links to information on many of the questions facing anyone planning for retirement. The "Money and Work" section in the Main Topics Area box takes you to links about many of the topics in this chapter. This is a site that deserves extensive exploration of its many links. Note especially within the "Money and Work" section the excellent discussion of reverse mortgages.

Medicare Website (www.medicare.gov) provides comprehensive information about current Medicare rules and guidelines and includes a downloadable version of *Medicare and You 2005.*

Morningstar (www.morningstar.com) is provided by Chicago-based Morningstar, Inc. which is a global investment research firm, offering an extensive line of products and services for individuals, financial advisors, institutions, and the media. Morningstar is an independent company that provides information, data, and analysis of stocks, mutual funds, exchange-traded funds, closed-end funds, and variable annuity/life sub-accounts. Much of the information on Morningstar is free, but one can subscribe to a premium account for about one hundred dollars a year that gives access to even more complete investing information.

Social Security Administration (www.ssa.gov) provides extensive information about Social Security benefits. By going to the section inside the top banner called "Benefits Planner," clicking on it, and then scrolling down to the section called "Calculators," you can make a quick estimate of what your Social Security benefit payments would be. Here you can change the variables to see what would happen if you retire at different ages, or with different final salaries.

Numerous investment and brokerage firms have their own web sites. Listed here are a few:

Fidelity Investments at (www.fidelity.com)

Oppenheimer Fund at (www.oppenheimerfunds.com)

Putnam Investment Management at (www.putman.com)

The Vanguard Group at (www.vanguard.com)

7

Personal Management Decisions for Your Sixties Decade

"People keep talking about retiring, and Social Security, and their 401-K accounts. I don't see what all the fuss is about. I certainly plan to keep working until I'm at least 70, if not longer, so I have nothing to worry about," said Joe Smith, a research chemist, in a conversation about his planning for his 60's.

While it is true that many people will continue to work through the entire decade of their 60's, either because they really enjoy their work or because they feel they need the income, there are still important personal management issues to plan for. And unless you've made a number of plans, a number of decisions, by your early 60's, you may find you've created significant problems for yourself and your loved ones later. This chapter will describe a number of these important decisions:

- creating an appropriate will,

- planning for disposition of your assets,

- deciding about appropriate medical insurance and life insurance,

- investigating long-term care insurance,

- making plans for interment, and

- dealing with needs of members of your family including aged parents, minor children, or disabled dependents.

Do you have a will? Every adult should have a will. You may think it isn't necessary because you don't have a large estate. However, think of the assets you have in your home, automobiles, insurance policies, etc. These can add up to a significant amount of money. If you don't have a will, the decisions you should be making about the distribution of your assets will be made by the laws of your state. And these laws will not necessarily respond to your personal wishes and family circumstances. For example, without a will, not all of your money will necessarily go to your spouse, even if you want it to. Part of the money may go to grown children, or more distant relatives. Possibly none of the money will go to stepchildren, even though you intended to include them in your legacy.

You may think that having a will really doesn't matter because you have put everything in joint ownership, so that when the first of the couple dies, everything is still owned by the second. But what if you die together? Then what decisions might you want to have made? If you have minor children, have you provided for the most appropriate plan of care for them if a tragedy hits both of you? All these problems can be dealt with by creating your will. This can be simple or complex. But it really must be done!

Still, many people avoid this topic. A recent article in *USA Today* reports that 74 percent of adults with minor children do not have a will. Those surveyed without wills listed one or more reasons for not having one: 40 percent don't have a will because they "don't have the time," 26 percent think "it's too expensive," 16 percent "don't like working with attorneys," another 15 percent "don't like facing death," and 27 percent "never thought of it." This avoidance is not really fair to your loved ones, and many unintended consequences can result from such poor planning.

Two real-life examples illustrate this. John and his brothers suddenly received $10,000 each from their deceased mother's brother. But their aunt, the sister of the man who had died, reported that the uncle had really wanted all his money to go to a cousin who was having serious financial difficulties. Because there was no will, the money was distributed in accord with state law, and the result was that the cousin received nothing.

Even where a will exists, poor planning can create problems. Delight recently received $25,000 from an aunt who had died following the death of her husband. They left their IRA monies to nieces and nephews, and the balance to The University of California at Berkeley. Unfortunately, because IRA monies are taxed as regular income, the heirs had to pay 28-38 percent of what they inherited in taxes. If the aunt had kept the same amount out of her other holdings, she could have left the bequests tax-free as part of her estate that can be passed on without estate taxes. She could have left the IRA money to the university, which would have paid no taxes as a non-profit institution. With a well-planned will, they could have left more to family and the same amount to the university.

With this statement Michael Palermo opens his introduction to his excellent web site *Crash Course in Wills and Trusts...the estate planning information you need:*

> Wills and Trusts are just tools in the larger process of estate planning. There is an unfortunate, widespread misconception that this is a subject of interest only to the wealthy. In fact, an

estate plan provides the legal mechanism for disposing of property upon death in a way that recognizes your wishes and the needs of your survivors, while minimizing taxes. For many it involves, even more importantly, planning for the handling of affairs in case of disability, and the deeply personal medical choices to be made as life nears its end. Estate planning is *not* just for rich people.

You can find the information about this site in the resources section.

In books and at web sites such as this you can find clear information on issues related to planning wills and trusts, as well as a basic process for constructing your own will on line. Palermo, however, cautions that a simple, do-it-yourself will may not deal with all the complexities of your actual situation. By following his process, you can begin the planning of your own will, but he recommends that, unless your situation is very simple, you should then have an attorney review your decisions and your will to make sure that all key contingencies are adequately dealt with, that your will does in fact accomplish your personal goals and that it complies with state law. But it is better to do a very simple will that you create yourself than not to do one at all.

Don't think that your family can just divide up what you have. They can't do it that easily. Friction can easily develop if family members have different ideas of your intentions about money, house, and personal possessions. A will makes your intentions clear and binding! The unintended consequences of poor planning can cause grieving. Delight's grandmother was bitter for years about "her family silver." She had given it to her older daughter when her older daughter married. But shortly after the wedding, the daughter died unexpectedly from heart failure, which originated in rheumatic fever she suffered as a child. Because the daughter left no will, the silver went to the new husband. He quickly remarried and the silver the grandmother had spent 50 years collecting for her daughters and granddaughters passed to strangers, never to be seen again. A will indicating distribution of possessions such as this silver can help during a time of great grief.

If you have minor children or a disabled adult dependant, be sure that a plan of care is clearly established in your will. If not, and if the worst should happen to both parents, the guardian responsibilities might pass to individuals whom you consider totally unsuitable to care for your children. In deciding on a plan, talk to the other people involved; talk to your children.

It is in this circumstance too that planning for a trust is important. You may not want to leave any financial assets directly to children, as they are then entitled to full control at the time they turn 18. Teenage children are usually not equipped to make major financial decisions for themselves. So planning for funds to be left in a trust may be an important part of developing a suitable will. And again, this isn't just for the very wealthy.

Beyond creating a will, then, you should plan a trust if your finances warrant it. In fact, a trust can be useful even if there are no minor children involved. In a simple case, one spouse leaves all assets to the other spouse. Then that spouse would make a will detailing where the assets would go upon his/her death. But it isn't as simple as that. Here we get into what are commonly called "death taxes" or federal estate taxes.

Each person can currently leave an unlimited amount to the other spouse, and can leave a total of 1.5 million dollars tax-free to any one person or a number of people combined. This amount rises slowly during the first decade of the twenty-first century, under current estate tax law. In 2006 it rises to 2 million, and in 2009 to 3.5 million. But here is the key point. If you die and leave everything to your spouse, and his/her estate is then worth more than 1.5 million dollars, that person's estate will have to pay significant taxes on everything beyond that first 1.5 million. But if each of you sets up a trust for your half of the amount of assets you hold, leaving income and usage to the other spouse, but directing the ultimate distribution beyond the spouse, you can avoid estate taxes on up to the second 1.5 million dollars. In 2005 that would have been a savings to your estate of more than half a million dollars.

This becomes significant if your joint assets will total more than 1.5 million dollars. Remember, that isn't too farfetched for many people. Houses, insurance, pensions, retirement accounts all add up to major asset holdings for many couples. Study just how much your joint estate is really worth, now and in the future, and decide if you should establish some trust vehicle. The basic rule of thumb should be that if all your assets combined are worth more than 1.5 million dollars, and if you want to direct these assets to your family or friends, you should establish a trust.

Or you may choose to leave a portion of your estate to a charitable organization. If you decide to do this, your estate planning may be very different and perhaps more simple. But do make the decisions, plan appropriately, and get a legally binding will produced. Then keep a copy and give a copy to a trusted friend, family member, or attorney, so that it can be found when needed.

Again, there are many sites on the World Wide Web that give excellent introductory information on this matter. The Palermo site given above has a good overview of the issues to consider.

Do you have appropriate insurance? Insurance is another area in which careful planning should take place at this time. The three major areas to consider are health insurance, life insurance, and long-term care insurance.

Health insurance. Once you turn 65, you are probably eligible for Medicare if you are eligible for Social Security whether or not you choose to retire. But, as discussed in the last chapter, many jobs do not pay in to Social Security so you may not qualify for Medicare. At least six months before you turn 65, and preferably much sooner, you should carefully research what is available and what you are eligible for, and begin the process of application. Usually people take out both Part A (hospital insurance) and Part B (doctor and outpatient care insurance) coverage, as that will increase what you receive in support. But Medicare does not cover many of the medical expenses older people face. If you are not in a group plan that provides comprehensive coverage after you retire, you may want to get supplemental coverage, which is available from a wide variety of sources. One place to begin research is through AARP (formerly the American Association of Retired Persons), which offers supplemental coverage, as well as some prescription assistance.

If you are covered by medical insurance at your current job, and you plan to retire, you may be eligible for continuation of your coverage for some months at your own expense. This is called COBRA coverage. Ask your human resources office if you are eligible for this coverage, and if so, for how many months and at what expense to you. Often this is the best coverage you will be able to find, but the maximum length of time most people can receive this coverage is 18 months after you leave your employment. So if you plan to retire before age 65, you can usually get the COBRA coverage for up to 18 months, but if that won't cover you up to the time you turn 65, you probably need to explore other means of medical coverage as well.

When Delight retired she chose to continue her Seattle University group health coverage under the provisions of the COBRA act. Given her previous health problems, she worried about continuing coverage when COBRA was scheduled to end. Her insurance agent gave her good advice. The agent said the coverage under COBRA was best, but when it came to an end, she would be able to arrange ongoing insurance. There were, however, certain requirements. Delight had to apply for the new coverage within sixty days of COBRA termination and not before. Also, the new coverage had to start immediately after COBRA ended. If there had been a gap, Delight would have been denied. Since Delight's COBRA was scheduled to end on June 30, she visited her agent again on May 1 to select the coverage and company she wanted. The agent completed the application and Delight's new policy went into effect July 1.

An excellent source of information about health insurance is maintained by the nonprofit Institute for Health Care Research and Policy at Georgetown University. Its web site is included in the resources at the end of this chapter. At this site you can find out about consumer guidelines for getting health insurance on a state-by-state basis.

Life insurance. Life insurance is another matter you'll need to consider. Life insurance for older people may be a major expense without too much return. However, if you have a young spouse, young children, or a disabled dependant, life insurance may be a good purchase.

At 68, Tim, whom we met in an earlier chapter, has two teenage children and a wife in her early 50's. Despite the cost, he chose to maintain a term-life policy even though his wife is a professional who is continuing to work. Jim, one of Delight's riding clinic friends, a consultant who spends about twenty-five days a month flying around the country, does not carry regular life insurance. But for a very low premium he carries coverage that would pay his wife if he were killed in a plane disaster.

Find out about premiums for your coverage, and decide whom you would want to receive the benefit. Are there other ways to invest that money that might be more supportive? Some people choose to get "term life" which is usually less expensive, but lasts for a certain number of years only. If the policy holder lives longer than the term, no money is paid out. This can be useful if, for example, you want to provide income for your children until they reach adulthood. Investigate insurance options carefully, and decide whether the investment is really the best place to put your money.

Long-term care insurance. Another major question you face in your fifties or sixties is whether you should buy long-term care insurance for yourself and/or your spouse. It is clearly debatable as to whether these policies are really useful and worth the money spent because the policy will only pay off if one is placed in a nursing facility or receiving home health care for a prolonged period of time. But as most of us live longer, this is a distinct possibility, and in today's society, support for medical care over the long term is not available to anyone with significant assets without private payment. Medicare pays only for a very short time of care after hospitalization and Medicaid covers only those without significant assets.

Delight pondered whether she should get long-term health care insurance. A widow with no children, she recognized that the last years of her life will be largely alone. Long-term insurance, which could cover a nursing home or in-home care, is an attractive option. But by the time she got around to applying, she was deemed ineligible because of hip surgeries and breast cancer. Had she started the process earlier, she might have been much more secure in planning for her own old age. However, as the years passed and she remained healthy, she was finally able to obtain long-term care insurance, albeit at a greater cost.

According to a *Consumer Reports* article in January, 2001, the need for assistance is increasing. "With the number of people who will need help with activities of daily living [ADLs] projected to increase by 51 percent in the next 20 years, assisted living is in a growth mode." So support is available, but it is expensive. That article goes on to say assisted living costs can exceed $4000 per month, and expenses are rising 3 to 5 percent per year. Full nursing home care is even more expensive, and estimates range from $30,000 to over $100,000 per year.

The six activities of daily living, commonly referred to as ADLs, upon which most long-term care insurance policies are based, are bathing, continence, dressing, eating, toileting and transferring. Typically, benefits are paid when a person is unable to perform a certain number of the ADLs, and is predicted to need assistance in performing them over a prolonged period of time, such as 90 days. Some policies may cover cognitive impairment. In selecting a policy, it is important to compare how many ADLs must require assistance for the policy to begin making payments.

What are your odds of needing long-term care insurance? That is the question. According to *A Shopper's Guide to Long-Term Care Insurance,* published by the National Association of Insurance Commissioners:

> It is difficult to predict who will need long-term care, but there are studies that help shed some light on the likelihood of needing such care. For example, one national study projects that 43 % of those people who turned age 65 in 1990 will enter a nursing home at some time during their life. The same study reported that among all persons who live to age 65, only 1 in 3 will spend three months or more in a nursing home; about 1 in 4 will spend one year or more in a nursing home; and only about 1 in 11 will spend five years or more in a nursing home. In other words, 2 out of 3 people who turned 65 in 1990 will either never spend any time in a nursing home or will spend less than three months in one.

If you have assets, most of these assets must then be used to pay for care before you become eligible for Medicaid, through which the government will provide for long-term nursing home care. Again, you want to look carefully at your personal circumstance and decide whether long-term care insurance is an area in which to put some resources.

Some advise that if you decide to purchase long-term care insurance, the best time to do this may be in your late fifties or early sixties because when you buy a policy, you will get a set annual premium that will continue as long as you pay (unless the premium changes for all in your category in your state). Because this premium is based on your age at the time you buy the policy, if you buy it when you are younger, the annual premium will be substantially less.

Jim, who has the life insurance policy for flying, also recently purchased long-term care coverage for himself and his much-younger wife. Because they both are involved in an active and potentially risky endeavor, he decided that the time had come to get coverage. He found that his coverage, since he is in his later 60s, is fairly expensive, but buying coverage for his 48-year-old wife is extremely cheap. A policy that covers both of them was selected as that also lowered the premiums.

A specific example from TIAA-CREF, a well-respected company, illustrates the choices. They demonstrate with a comparison of three plans:

Benefits summary	Plan HA–99	Plan HB–99	Plan HC–99
Lifetime maximum benefits	$109,500	$182,500	Unlimited
Benefit period (maximum amount of time you would receive benefit)	3 Years	5 Years	Unlimited
Nursing facility Daily Care Benefit maximum	$100/day	$100/day	$100/day
Home and community care daily maximum	$100/day	$100/day	$100/day
Benefit waiting period	90 days	90 days	90 days
Periodic inflation Protection	Offered annually	Offered annually	Offered annually

The monthly payment for each of these plans varies by the age of the applicant. For example, the following chart indicates the variety of payments in a recent year.

Age at which one begins coverage	Monthly payment HA-99	Monthly payment HB – 99	Monthly payment HC – 99
Age 55	$35.05	$43.09	$58.98
Age 60	$49.58	$60.69	$80.36
Age 65	$70.95	$86.34	$111.99
Age 70	$108.57	130.79	$166.70

To see what this actually means in dollars spent, let us assume that Tom Smith gets an HC-99 policy when he is 55 and pays regularly until he needs nursing care at age 80. He will have paid a total of $17,694.00 in premiums. Robert Jones, however, waits until he is 70 to purchase the same policy (assuming he is still healthy and able to get the policy) and then also needs nursing home care when he turns 80. He will have paid $20,004.00 in premiums.

A wide variety of long-term care policies are available. In addition to your age and the lifetime maximum benefits you select, a number of other factors affect cost and coverage. Some of those variables are how long the coverage will last (e.g., one year, three years, for as long as you need it), whether it includes in-home care, the amount per day that will be paid out and whether there is an inflation factor built in so that each year your coverage will go up to cover increases in the cost of care. For example, daily payments can range from a low of around $50 to $300 or more.

Another factor is the deductible you accept. The deductible is the number of days you will pay your own long-term care costs before the insurance will start paying. The longer your deductible, the lower the premium you will pay. You can say you want the coverage to start immediately, after 20 days of care, or up to after a year of care. The premiums vary substantially based on this decision. One expert has recommended choosing a policy that pays out $150 per day, has a 5% inflation factor, and starts after 90 days of care has been received. This would mean you would have to pay the first continuous 90 days out of your own pocket before the insurance would begin to cover you.

The other key item to verify in selecting the policy is what condition makes you eligible to receive coverage. Many policies will say that before you can get coverage, you must need constant assistance for some of the six daily needs. You want a policy that comes into effect after one or two of the six daily needs actually require assistance.

So long-term care insurance is an issue that needs careful consideration and a good decision while you are still in good health. Once you have developed serious medical problems, as Delight has, it is probably too late to get this coverage, at least immediately or at reasonable cost.

AARP (formerly the American Association for Retired Persons) sums up the key points that should be included in a good long-term care policy as follows:

- Does not require prior hospitalization to receive benefits.

- Is guaranteed renewable as long as you pay the premiums. This does not mean that premiums cannot be raised.

- Offers a premium waiver while you are receiving benefits.

- Has one deductible for the life of the policy.

- Covers pre-existing conditions, without a waiting period, if these are disclosed when you apply.

- Offers five percent (5%) compound inflation protection.

- Allows policyholders to upgrade or downgrade their coverage if they cannot afford premiums.

So, do you have enough assets for long-term care? Can you anticipate seeing a member of your family live for ten years after being disabled by a stroke, as Edith did?

A widow, Edith lived on her own until she was 88. Her financial support came from her late husband's Social Security and her savings. Then she suffered the stroke and moved to her daughter's home. Although therapy helped her improve at first, her condition gradually deteriorated and she eventually moved into a private room in a nursing home near her daughter. When her small savings ran out and she could no longer afford the nursing home fees, she applied for and received Medicaid, turning her Social Security payments over to the state. She was able to remain in the same nursing home, but she was moved into a room with two other patients. Unlike many others in the home, she had daily visits from faithful family members throughout the eight years that she lived there.

Do you have enough assets to keep yourself and/or your spouse in long-term care? Sometimes it may be for a short period, but for some this is 10-15 years. Do you mind spending down your own assets, for example selling your home and using the proceeds, to pay for care? If assets are depleted, are you comfortable using Medicaid? What is your family genetic history? Are there people in your immediate family who have required care for a prolonged period of time? All these questions should be carefully considered as you make decisions about long-term care. But if you think you wish to purchase this kind of coverage, do not wait until you need it. Then you probably won't be able to get it!

What planning is needed for loved ones? Another decision you may need to make in the decade of your sixties concerns planning for care for your elderly loved ones. You may have one or more parents, other relatives or dear friends who are in their eighties or nineties and who may need special attention or support. In fact, concern over care of an ill father was a key factor leading Julie to retire early.

No one in Julie's family had anticipated that her father would outlive her mother, but he did. At 88, he was able to stay in the family home on his own for three years, until a combination of health problems caused him to require in-home care. Julie made the one-hour drive to see him once or twice a week. He had good care-givers and good neighbors, but when he began to require 24-hour care, it became difficult to find adequate help. After Julie retired, he lived at Julie's on a trial basis for awhile but found it lonely. Good senior centers offering day care and a variety of activities were nearby, but he had lost interest in having new experiences. Eventually, with encouragement from his Masonic friends, he chose to move to the assisted-living area in a retirement home belonging to that organization, also about an hour away from Julie's. As his health deteriorated further and his care involved more of her time, she was happy that she had retired.

Careful plans for care must be made with the individual's wishes in mind, but also with recognition of what is realistic. Many older people want to remain in their own homes. Is this really appropriate? Sometimes it is easier to assist elderly people to relocate while they are still able to adjust easily to changes in their environment. Should your parents leave their home of many years and move into a retirement community? Will they need assistance? Will they be willing to discuss these issues and make appropriate plans? This is a very delicate area for discussion and decision-making, but planning before a crisis emerges often makes the process easier.

Marla Kranz, who was concerned about her elderly parents who lived several states away and refused to move closer, was advised to invite them for a long holiday visit. This allowed them to adjust to the idea of relocating without forcing the decision in advance of a permanent move.

What planning is needed for death? Finally, there is the difficult planning that should take place around your own death. There are two major questions to face while you are physically and mentally capable of appropriate decisions. The first is the need for a "Living Will" or medical directive. This instrument clearly lays out your personal wishes about such things as being maintained on life support systems, etc. You must decide whether you wish to remain alive at all costs, utilizing major medical interventions, or whether you wish to die in a more natural way. This problem can be terrible for your loved ones if you haven't stated your wishes clearly.

Jennifer was faced with bringing her husband to the emergency room with a raging fever and delirium. Recognizing that this could become a life-and-death situation, the emergency room doctor asked for directions regarding last wishes. Knowing that her husband had left a living will stating that no major efforts were to be made to sustain a life on support systems, she replied that some attempts should be made to revive him if it came to that, but no ventilator or extreme measures should be used to prolong a coma or terminal life. The doctor, however, responded that she couldn't have it both ways. Either efforts would be made to revive him, and all efforts would be made, or else no efforts would be made.

This seems harsh, but there is a clear decision that needs to be made—should all efforts to keep a person alive be made or should the person be able to die peacefully, if that is the individual's will? This may vary from state to state, hospital to hospital, and doctor to doctor.

This terribly difficult decision must be made, and discussed, long before an emergency arises. You must let others know what your true wishes are. And that conversation can be hard. Recently Marcia, a very active woman in her late seventies, related a conversation she tried to have with her daughter. She started to tell about her wishes, and the daughter cut her off with, "Mother, I won't have this depressing conversation." The discussion ended there, without Marcia being allowed to honestly state her personal preferences about a situation that will, in reality, face many of us. Having a living will both makes your wishes known and provides a vehicle for an honest conversation about this painful subject.

The American Medical Association provides a very good web site that contains a question-and-answer section as well as a draft Living Will form that can be copied and completed. The site is given in the resources at the end of this chapter.

Another difficult topic to be faced is your wish regarding interment. Do you want to be buried or cremated? Do you have a plot chosen? Again, making up your own mind and then letting your wishes be known are very important at this stage in your life. The plan you make should be written clearly and left with your will, so that others will be able to follow your directions at a very emotional time.

You might choose to draft a simple letter, saying something like this:

> Dear_____,
>
> You have long been a trusted friend, so I am asking you to take responsibility for this difficult task.
>
> I wish to be cremated, my ashes spread on the water we have enjoyed together, and I want a simple memorial service that includes family and the following close friends only.
>
> Yours, _____

Or you might choose to give very different instructions about a church mass and burial in a specific gravesite. You may wish to indicate whether you wish your body or organs to be donated for transplant, for research, or for educational purposes.

The key point is that you should make decisions about your own personal wishes, and clearly communicate these decisions to your loved ones. Do not make them face a set of hard choices at this difficult time without guidance from you. Remember, members of your family may have differing opinions. By not stating your own wishes, you are laying open a possibility of major tensions at this emotional time!

Money is one of the questions that we all face as we age. But the question of finances in the last third of one's life is only one of the major personal management questions that must be recognized and planned for in order to have a smooth aging period. The question of planning an appropriate will and estate, recognizing the role of various types of insurance in older life, and planning for the end of life must all be faced. And these decisions can be made most gracefully at a time when they are not acute crises. Take time when you are well, healthy, and happy to make these decisions that will affect you and your loved ones as you age.

RESOURCES

There are many excellent sources of information on issues raised in this chapter; only a few are given below as a suggested starting place for further research and reading on the topics of financial planning for your sixties and beyond.

Books:

Bamford, J., et al. (2000). *The Consumer Reports Money Book (3rd edition)*. New York: Consumer Reports. This book provides an excellent introduction to many of the topics of money management and personal affairs planning.

Clifford, D. & Jordan, C. (2002). *Plan Your Estate (6th edition)*. Berkeley: Nolo. Another excellent book from Nolo, this covers the basics of tax-saving strategies, wills and living trusts, the many other kinds of trusts, as well as the variety of estate planning options available. Written in plain English, it gives information that can help one make important decisions and have the background knowledge that will help in an estate-planning meeting with a lawyer.

Hannon, K. (2000). *Getting Started in Estate Planning*. New York: John Wiley and Sons. This book gives an excellent introduction to the many issues surrounding estate planning. Written in a clear and concise style, the book provides guidance to those who need to begin the process of planning for their own wishes to be carried out after death.

Hughes, T. and Klein, D. (2001). *A Family Guide to Wills, Funerals, and Probate. (2nd edition)*. New York: Checkmark Books. This book effectively explains wills and how they function, provides many examples, worksheets, and checklists for planning, and allows one to understand the decisions that need to be made, either independently or in conjunction with a lawyer.

Quinn, J. (1998). *Making the Most of Your Money, Completely Revised and Updated for the Twenty-First Century*. New York: Simon and Schuster. While this book is getting a little old, it is an encyclopedic handbook of chapters dealing with most of the key issues of financial planning for one's future and for one's estate. If there is one reference to have on the topic of financial planning, this might be the one.

Sitarz, D. (2000). *Prepare Your Own Will, The National Will Kit (5th edition)*. Carbondale, Il: Nova. This is a step-by-step workbook which provides simplified legal forms, detailed instructions, questionnaires, checklists and sample wills. It would be possible to develop a will and other legal documents independently by following the instructions in this book.

Tobias, A. (2002). *The Only Investment Guide You'll Ever Need, Expanded and Updated*, San Diego: Harvest. Understanding your money, your budget, and your possible investments is the goal of this book. Most aspects of personal finance, including spending, investing, insurance, who you can trust to handle your money, and tax strategies are all discussed in an engaging style. This is an easily read book on the topic of finances.

Web Sites:

AARP (formerly the American Association of Retired Persons) (www.aarp.org) will lead you to AARP's basic web site where there are many excellent links for further information on many of the questions to be faced in retirement planning.

American Medical Association (www.ama-assn.org/public/booklets/ livgwill.htm) has a very useful question and answer section plus sample forms on living wills that can be printed and completed. Most useful is "Shape Your Health Care Future with HEALTH CARE ADVANCE DIRECTIVES" which was developed jointly by the American Association of Retired Persons, the American Bar Association Commission on Legal Problems of the Elderly, and the American Medical Association (www.abanet.org/lawinfo/adb.pdf). The booklet contains a good overview of Advance Care Directives, followed by a form and instructions that can be printed and completed.

Institute for Health Care Research and Policy at Georgetown University (www.healthinsuranceinfo.net) is an excellent site for information available on a state-by-state basis, about health insurance policies and guidelines.

National Association of Insurance Commissioners (www.naic.org). This site contains a great deal of valuable information on insurance, with information given on a state-by-state basis. Their publication "A Shopper's Guide to Long-Term Care

Insurance" can be found at www.yourlongtermcare.com/pdfs/
NAIC_vol_991.pdf.

The Nolo.com Self-Help Law Center (www.nolo.com). At this site
you can download or order will and trust-writing software. It
has excellent information on legal and tax issues.

Palermo, M.T. (www.mtpalermo.com) "Crash Course in Wills and
Trusts…the estate planning information you need." This site
has very complete information on wills, trusts, and living wills.
It includes ways to create a will and a living trust on the internet for a fee.

8

The Time of the Rest of Your Life

September 26 was the birthday of Texan Connie Douglas Reeves, and she usually spent some part of that day on the back of her horse, Dr. Pepper. Despite her limp, a legacy of Dr. Pepper's kick to her thigh in 1986, and the fact that she was born in 1901, she was still riding nearly every day 101 years later. She was still teaching riding, too, although she said she couldn't see much and didn't hear very well either.

Dr. Mel Bleakney celebrated his 100th birthday in August of 2002, a week after returning from an Alaskan fishing trip. A month later he was saluted during a University of Washington football game for his record of 73 years as a season-ticket holder.

At last report, life expectancy for Americans is around 77 years, and it continues to increase. Over half of those in the baby boom generation can expect to live at least into their mid-eighties; by 2050 there may be as many as a million Americans who are 100 or older. In other words, whatever your image of the sixty-year-old, the fact is that on average, that person still has a lot of living to do. Furthermore, he or she is likely to enjoy relatively good physical and mental health and relative financial security. The key word of course is "relative." At least until the Fountain of Youth is discovered, we will all continue to deteriorate physically as we age, and the financial future is always uncertain. Nevertheless, increased knowledge and technology for maintaining health and the national commitment to some form of life-long financial support give us the prospect of a better life, and for longer, than any previous generation.

The task for 60-year-olds, then, is to make the most of the next 25 or 30 years. That raises a host of issues, many of which have been topics of earlier chapters—when to retire, how to have enough to live on when you do, how to take care of your body and your mind, your connection to family and friends.

What kind of life will you make? Tying all these practical matters together is a fundamental question. How will you spend those years, what direction will you choose for the last third of your life? Of course you need to address the basics—health, relationships, money—but you have the opportunity to pay much deeper attention to life quality and meaning than most of us do during our working years.

On the surface this may appear to be a simple matter of deciding how to use your time once earning a living no longer occupies such a large chunk of it. Even for those who continue to work in their sixties and beyond, the sense of time fleeting is likely to stimulate more thoughtfulness on how it is spent. Yet underlying this surface issue is something more fundamental. You may call it attitude, or self-image, or adaptation, or what you will. It is the way you see yourself and the world around you, and whatever you call it, it is key to the satisfaction you will enjoy during this last third of your life.

Are we talking about changing yourself? Perhaps; but to some extent it may happen without conscious effort, as part of the natural adult development process. Researchers have found little change in many aspects of adult experience and personality. But long-term studies also show that people do see change "in their own attitudes, in self-esteem, and in how aware they are of their own ideas, beliefs, and attitudes." The most dramatic changes are reported "in how we see ourselves and in how we feel about ourselves, others, and life."

You read in the chapter on mental health how a positive attitude contributes to longevity. In *Aging Well*, George Vaillant lists attitudinal characteristics that are common among healthy 75-to-80-year-olds. The list includes being hopeful and open to new ideas, caring about and for others, retaining a sense of humor, taking sustenance from the past yet learning from the next generation, being tolerant of one's own faults and forgiving of those around you. Taken together, they suggest an approach to the world that contributes to our mental and therefore also to our physical well-being, and that has importance for the ways we use our time in these next decades.

Janet is a poster woman for these characteristics. At 84, she is full of energy, both physical and creative. A lifelong educator, she has launched many innovative programs to improve educational opportunities for disadvantaged urban youth. She continues to help many young educators advance their careers and she stays current with new ideas. Janet keeps up with her children and grandchildren, walks two miles each day and remains active in her profession.

What are some resources for positive change? Cognitive psychology, currently the fastest growing of the non-pharmaceutical therapies, provides practical methods for improving your outlook on life. Martin Seligman, whose book on *Learned Optimism* was cited in the chapter on mental health, has recently written another book in this field entitled *Authentic Happiness*. As the title suggests, Seligman offers techniques, backed up with evidence from research, for using his "Positive Psychology" to increase personal fulfillment. He suggests means of achieving greater satisfaction from the past, optimism for the future, and happiness in the present. Seligman's descriptions of two avenues to happiness are relevant for our exploration of choices. He describes <u>gratifications</u> as endeavors that totally absorb us and involve us in expressing our personal strengths and values. He contrasts these pursuits with <u>pleasures</u>, which appeal to the senses and emotions, and he suggests it is gratifications that produce psychological growth and the foundation for genuine and lasting happiness.

This is thought-provoking for the person contemplating choices about how to use the time of the sixties and beyond. Given what we know about the connection between attitude and successful aging, it's worth your while to take time out during this decade for some serious introspection about the direction your life is taking. What do you value? What are your strengths? What parts of your life experience are most significant for you, engage you most powerfully? However you answer these questions, it's important to ask them and to let the answer guide your choices if you want to make the moments count.

Seligman offers a helpful framework for this in his examination of how to achieve happiness in the present. He makes a reasoned case for gratifications as the basis of deep happiness, and he sees the source of gratifications in identifying and acting on our "signature strengths." He concludes that the good life consists in "using your signature strengths every day in the main realms of your life to bring abundant gratification and authentic happiness."

According to Seligman, strengths that lead to gratification are those based on character traits that are recognized as virtues across time and across cultures. Using a classification system developed by a group of psychologists, he identifies six such characteristics: wisdom and knowledge, courage, love and humanity, justice, temperance, spirituality and transcendence. He then lists 24 strengths, each contributing to one of these virtues. He offers a way to identify your strengths and then gives examples to show how you can employ and emphasize your own strengths in every aspect of your life. He suggests that strengths are not necessarily innate, like talents, but can be learned; choosing to acquire a given strength is an act of will.

Characteristics that Seligman lists as contributing to wisdom and knowledge, for example, include curiosity and interest in the world; love of learning; judgment and open-mindedness; ingenuity and originality; social, personal and emotional intelligence; and perspective. He describes the strengths related to each of the virtues in terms that enable you to determine whether and to what extent you possess them. To help you recognize your signature strengths, *Authentic Happiness* provides a brief test, and a more in-depth test is available on Seligman's web site. Before you read further, you might want to take the on-line test at www.authentichappiness.org.

There are a number of other well-known and widely tested measures of individual strengths, including the Myers-Briggs Type Indicator and the Strong Interest Inventory. Taking one of these instruments as you enter your sixties, even if you have done it at an earlier age, can be a valuable reminder of where your strengths lie. It might even surprise you, as it did Susan.

Susan has tried her hand at a number of entrepreneurial projects such as selling cosmetics and clothing at home parties since leaving a career as a teacher. When she took Seligman's test online, she discovered that by far her greatest strength was "zest, energy and enthusiasm."

Compared to others who have taken the test, she scored very high on this strength while scoring lower than she expected in other areas such as perseverance and diligence. Analyzing this, she realized that her zest and energy, while high, are somewhat unfocussed. That led her to consider how she might channel the energy more effectively, or accept that her strength lies in starting new projects but not necessarily staying with them very long. Since first taking the test, Susan has used it again to find acceptance for her habit of taking on too many of her friends' problems. She has decided that another strength is generosity of spirit, and that's a good thing—she just needs to develop a little more balance.

What are some of the options? As you consider choosing the richest ways of spending the precious capital of your time, why not sit down and make an inventory of the things you do that bring you the most gratification, that are so absorbing you forget about time passing, that call out your greatest strengths. Then think about how you can express your strengths in more of your activities, and think of other activities that will enable you to exercise your strengths.

Make no mistake: there is a wealth of choices. Volunteering, going back to school, traveling, taking up artistic or musical or theatrical pursuits, gardening, painting, cooking, woodworking, not to mention caring for grandchildren and aging parents—there is an endless array of people, activities and organizations ready to draw you into their orbit. One retired person's first piece of advice to a new retiree was, "Get ready to say, 'No.' As soon as people find out you're retired, they'll want your time."

Better yet, have a clear idea of what you want to say "Yes" to, and you'll be too busy to have a problem saying "No" to things you don't really want to do. Chuck is a sixty-two-year-old insurance agent who wasn't sure he wanted to retire but decided to try it for a year to see if he liked it. He found out pretty quickly that he liked it a lot, and he never looked back. But, he says, "I work at retirement. I make it a full-time job." As it happens, he finds his gratification in being a well-appreciated grandfather—and playing golf well at the inexpensive public course in his town. He knows what he wants to do, and he has no guilt about what he doesn't want to do. As Guild Fetridge says in *The Adventure of Retirement*, the key is to "be prepared to work at making retirement a success." Substitute "the next 30 years" for "retirement" in that statement and it fits every sixty-year-old, including those who've never held a job outside the home.

So what are the options? An obvious one is not to retire but to continue working, preferably at a job you enjoy or a new challenge that still brings you satisfaction along with earning money. As noted, this option appears to be especially attractive to women who may have entered a career later in life and still enjoy the sense of accomplishment as well as the social life a job provides. Many men, too, are drawn, or forced by finances, to stay in the job market. When a recession followed the bursting of the dot.com bubble in 2001-2002, a phenomenon of "un-retiring" emerged, as people whose retirement funds were invested in the stock market saw their financial future darken. If this happens to you, now is the time to examine your signature strengths and go into or stay with the kind of work that calls on those strengths and provides you with some measure of gratification.

You should be so lucky as to love your work as much as Selma Koch. Until the week before she died at 95, after breaking her hip in a fall, she worked 10 hours a day, six days a week. Her job? Selling lingerie to New Yorkers in the Town Shop, beginning in 1927 when she married the shop owner. She gained fame as the Bra Lady, who took pride in her ability to tell a woman's bra size just by looking. Serving the daughters and granddaughters of her first customers throughout her long life continued to gratify Mrs. Koch, whose obituary quoted her as having said, "No sales pressure—that we don't allow. The whole secret is having a relationship with people."

Again, as noted earlier, many people retire from a salaried position to go into business on their own. According to Fetridge, "as many as 20 percent of the over one million business startups each year are initiated by men and women fifty or over." This clearly is an area where you can—and should—choose a business that brings out your strong points, that gives you satisfaction to repay you for the long hours and insecurity that go along with being a small business owner.

Your own business could be one that provides consulting services to your former employer or others in your career field. This is a way to use knowledge and experience you gained during your career but to have more control of your time and earnings. Of course, it also means you have to be prepared to market your services as well as providing them, which introduces a set of challenges you may not have faced in a salaried position. If you have developed a strong network of professional colleagues during your career, now is the time to pull out your Rolodex or Palm Pilot and let them know you're available and interested in some independent assignments.

High on many people's lists for the golden years is spending time with family. This can be a welcome chance to stay involved in the lives of your children, perhaps even to make up for whatever regrets you harbor about your own parenting and to enjoy the unconditional love and high enthusiasm of young children. It's also a time to connect with other relatives you may have lost touch with or would like more contact with. Early in retirement John scanned into his computer family photos from four generations, edited and titled them, and produced an 8-CD set. The set also included a family genealogy back to the 1600s. Over 30 families spread across the country requested and received sets of the photo CDs. As a result, family members regularly call or email him about family history issues. Julie buys everything using a credit card that gives her frequent flyer miles, to help enable her to visit far-flung children and grandchildren. With a son who lives across the country with his wife and four children, and a daughter in Australia with two children, she looks for every opportunity to see them. Finding that adult children forgive the errors of their parents and appreciate having loving grandparents for their children is the greatest joy of these years for her.

Time with family can often mean providing a safety net for your parents, other elderly relatives, or grandchildren whose parents are working. A reality for many people is the need to care for a partner who has become disabled. This may be a difficult responsibility, disrupting plans for enjoying these years together. If this is the case, one resource could be to go to your repertoire of strengths to see if there is a way to exercise one or more of them and bring gratification into this corner of your life.

One well-known person who has clearly drawn on a number of strengths is Dana Reeve, now the widow of actor Christopher Reeve. After her husband was paralyzed in a riding accident, her life changed drastically. In one interview, she talked realistically about the changes. While not making light of them, she found value in "entering a world where you see the gift behind disability" and in the "intensity to life and relationships." Clearly, over the nine years her husband lived after the accident. Dana Reeve exhibited strengths in perseverance, courage and loving through her care-giving and their activities on behalf of disabled people. For her part, she found wisdom in this quotation from a book by Rosalynn Carter: "There are only four kinds of people: those who have been caregivers; those who are currently caregivers; those who will be caregivers; and those who will need caregivers." Carter's comment proved prescient when after Christopher's death, Dana announced that she had lung cancer.

Few caregivers have the attention and the financial resources of Dana Reeve, but all of them must rely on inner strength to sustain their work. Stanley is an engineer who spent ten years caring for his wife as she slowly withered from Parkinson's disease. Along with a loving heart and perseverance, Stanley called on his love of learning, becoming an expert on options for treatment and possibilities for cure of Parkinson's. Doing so also opened up an array of supporters through his exploration of the subject on the Internet.

If one of your signature strengths is a love of learning, there is an endless array of opportunities for you to go back to school, from taking a computer class at your local senior center or community college to earning a PhD. in German literature, as one seventy-year-old we know did after the grandchildren she cared for had started school. She wound up using her education when she got a part-time faculty appointment in the language department of a local college. The college students loved having an instructor who was not only a native speaker but could relate stories of life in Germany before World War II.

In some states, tuition for college classes is low or non-existent for seniors; community centers and public schools often have classes in current events, governmental affairs, hobbies and crafts. Andy, the retired longshoreman, calls himself "a course junky." He regularly takes three courses at a time under the low-tuition option at the university in his city. He has studied history and political science and is moving on to philosophy, and he loves the day his mail brings the next term's course catalog, opening up another menu of opportunities to learn.

The Chautauqua Institute and Elderhostel are just two of a number of organizations that cater to mature adults who are curious and want to continue their learning. Elderhostel programs in fact are expressly for those 55 and older; Chautauqua also offers special sessions for the over-55. These organizations offer residential programs focusing on history, arts, current issues, culture and a host of other topical areas. Many colleges and universities offer on-campus lecture-study programs open to seniors during regular college vacation periods. Senior citizen centers are an excellent source of free or low-cost lecture programs and classes in crafts, computer skills, and foreign language conversation, among others.

On the other hand, you may have knowledge or experiences that are worth sharing with others. If so, why not write a book or an article?

You might take inspiration from Delight's father, Robert Carter, who at 87 began translating the World War I diary of a German medical officer. Carter did it, he says, "for something to exercise my mind," not thinking of publishing it. A university professor encouraged him to publish his work, and now Carter's translation is in print, entitled "Tagebuch Im Kriege: A Diary of WWI Rumania." An early retiree, he opted out of the insurance business to enjoy a second career running a sailboat for charter before retiring a second time and eventually turning his hand to translation. This was not Carter's first foray into authorship; at 63, he wrote and published an account of life as a charter skipper, "Sail Far Away."

Painting, drawing, sculpting, ceramics—for the person with artistic leanings, intense gratification can come when you have the time to pursue your favorite art or craft.

Charlotte retired at 62 from a satisfying but consuming career as a college administrator. She had always wanted to paint but the demands of her job made it unrealistic even to consider trying to learn. Because she had found so much gratification in her work, she wasn't sure how she would adjust to retirement, but she knew she would start taking painting lessons. Like Chuck, once she took the step, she never looked back, and she is preparing to mount the first public show of her work. She lives Seligman's theory, for once she goes into her studio, she is completely engrossed, open to no distraction except from her well-fed cats.

The story of Ed's retirement is very much like Charlotte's. He was a popular pharmacist who reluctantly retired in his seventies, then realized that he finally had time to take up sculpting, which he had always wanted to do. He found a teacher who was just right for him, joined the class, and now he's another retiree with an absorbing, gratifying activity and works of art that amaze his family and friends.

For a better-known example, consider Anna Mary Robertson Moses, a home-maker who began painting in her late seventies after raising five children. Actually, she first took up embroidery but turned to painting when arthritis made it too painful to hold a needle. She had her first one-woman show when she was 80 and became famous as Grandma Moses. She lived to be 101 and in her last 20 years created more than 1600 works of art.

Then there is physical activity in one of a multitude of exercise programs for seniors offered by city recreation centers, YMCAs, YMHAs and commercial gyms. Group Health Cooperative, a health maintenance organization in the state of Washington, is an example of a health organization which provides free wellness programs and encourages participation by senior members. If you prefer to build your stamina and your bones more naturally, you'll find classes and clubs that offer lessons and guided excursions in hiking, skiing, mountain-climbing, running and yes, square-dancing—all active avenues to a toned body and a supple mind.

Until her death at 90, Doris indulged her love of opera, continued to work on a history of the classical music scene in her city, and still had time to run in senior races in her area and across the country. True, she was blessed with a slim, wiry body, but its maintenance was to her credit. Each of these activities brought out her signature strengths and gave her deep gratification.

If you love sports, you don't necessarily have to give them up at sixty, though you may gradually change what or how you play. Milton Katims, the esteemed former conductor of the Seattle Symphony Orchestra, offered his take on the subject in a newspaper interview on his 95th birthday. Asked about his secrets for long life, he had several pieces of advice, including "Stay married" and "Get lots of sleep." He also suggested finding a lifetime sport, one that you can keep doing for most of your life, and then adapting the sport as you age. Tennis was his choice, but there are even many men and women in their seventies and eighties who are still skiing. One lifelong enthusiast who is still a ski instructor at 85 explained how he adapted this way: "My wife made me stop racing at 75."

Less risky alternatives like jogging, hiking and walking can also give you pleasure and companionship if you want it, for many years.

How about making a difference for others? Another big category of activities that can provide intense gratification is volunteering. From the Peace Corps to tutoring in your neighborhood school, the possibilities are nearly endless. Fetridge reports that about 10 percent of Peace Corps volunteers today are over 55. Star of this group is Miss Lillian Carter, mother of the former president. As a young woman, she had trained and worked as a nurse, so when she was 68 she volunteered and spent a term using her nursing skills among the poor in India.

Just about every non-profit organization can use free clerical and technical experts, caregivers of all kinds, fund-raisers (always!), and board members. Schools use volunteers in classrooms, the library, the playground and the crosswalks. For art lovers and natural history buffs, the training to be a docent in a museum is an opportunity in itself, and sharing what you learn with museum-goers offers another kind of gratification. Hospital volunteers run the gift shops and entertain in children's wards. Many international aid organizations need physicians, dentists and other retired professionals for short-term service in Third World countries where the rewards in gratitude and goodwill are priceless. Julie's husband, Gordon, volunteered to spend a week giving dental care to families in Oaxaca, Mexico, and found the experience so satisfying and the need so great that he signed up to go again later the same year. These same organizations also need just plain laborers–anyone who will lend a hand in pouring concrete floors, digging wells, and other work to improve life for impoverished people. And while this work overseas usually involves paying your own travel expenses, there are many opportunities here at home that cost only your time. For example, you could help such organizations as Habitat for Humanity build houses for low-income families.

The Executive Service Corps (ESC) is a good resource for retired professionals who would like to continue employing their expertise. ESC serves as a broker between professionals interested in volunteering as consultants and non-profit organizations, including schools, colleges, churches and healthcare agencies, looking for experts in specific areas. Demand is high for such skills as accounting, marketing, organizational development and communication. Ralph and John, retired executives from a major computer firm, have spent several gratifying years advising a technical institute as members of ESC. That experience led to an invitation to provide similar consultation in eastern Europe.

Some charitable umbrella organizations also broker volunteer services. For example, the United Way of King County, Washington, has a Volunteer Center that connects volunteers and organizations seeking volunteers. The center has a web site where people can learn about volunteer opportunities. Other United Way organizations may offer similar services; check to see if one is available in your city or county.

Alongside the spiritual dimension, which is the subject of the next chapter, involvement in a religious congregation also offers a wealth of opportunities for volunteer service. Most religious organizations welcome participation in teaching young people or advising their activities, taking care of the physical plant, and engaging in the outreach and charitable activities centered around religious life. Rewards that come from these activities are not only personal gratification and recognition from fellow members of the congregation, but also the social relationships that usually result from such involvement.

Have you always thought you'd like to run for political office? Now's your chance. Start out as a precinct committee person or campaign volunteer, and if you express interest in being a candidate, you may well find yourself on your party's ticket before you know it. American political parties are looking for good people to fill many positions, and that could give you an opportunity to employ several of your signature strengths in an absorbing endeavor. Sometimes, it's true, you may be the token candidate in a hopeless race for a seat that's safely in another party's pocket. Making a good run as a sacrificial lamb, though, can lead to exposure and earn the loyalty of your party, which could bring you a shot at a more viable race. As for the age factor, you can make your own list of popular and effective legislators and other officials who have served well past their sixties.

Independent activism has brought satisfaction to the lives of many people when they retire. A poster woman for the joy of activism would be Hazel Wolf, 1898 to 2000. Celebrated in one of Studs Terkel's books, she was an activist all her life. At 100, she was still editing an environmental newsletter and was noted for her humor and wisdom as well as for her determined championing of social and environmental issues from "the rights of workers, women, prisoners and minorities to the need for wilderness, wetlands, wild life and world peace." A single mother, she worked as a legal secretary until retiring at 67. She then began to work with the Audubon Society and before she was through, had started 20 chapters of the Society in the Pacific Northwest, Canada and Russia and had led numerous environmental battles.

On a more modest scale, Julie's mother threw her considerable energy into activism after raising her children and retiring from 25 years of work in the state employment security office. In her 60s by then, she joined a campaign that succeeded in stopping a nuclear plant that was proposed near an earthquake-prone fault line in her county. In the process, she gained new friends and respect for the different lifestyles of her much younger compatriots. That led her to participate with these young counter-culturists in founding a food cooperative, which fit perfectly with her lifelong interest in healthy diet.

Travel is one of the activities Americans most commonly look forward to when they are freed from the constraints of a job. Here the possibilities are endless, as are the organizations ready to help you make your dreams come true. The American Automobile Association and similar organizations in many other countries will advise you if you want to go on your own, or offer economical packages if you want someone else to do the planning. Elderhostel, an easy way to travel and learn, is also relatively economical. For a more deluxe experience, many universities and their alumni associations now promote trips with noted faculty leading tours in their area of research. When China and India were still considered off the beaten path for tourists, Althea and Harold traveled to both countries on well-organized and comfortable tours sponsored by their alma mater. The travelers learned about history, culture and geography of the countries from popular professors and visited areas not on the usual tourist itineraries.

Then there are the new American gypsies, the couples with their dog traveling the highways in their recreational vehicle complete with a compact car tagging along, stopping wherever they like—and wherever they can find a camping spot in a state park or a KOA campground. The economics of RV travel may not quite pencil out when you factor in fuel, maintenance and insurance along with initial cost, but they give a certain kind of freedom for taking your own time, stopping whenever you like and yet carrying something of home with you.

In sum: There is no reason for people in their sixties who are in reasonable health to be bored. Possibilities range from activities that cost nothing except your time—like volunteering or joining a book club at your local library—to taking a five-star cruise through the Greek Islands. In Seligman's picture of happiness, any of these activities may bring you either fleeting pleasure or deep gratification, depending on how much of your signature strengths you bring to them. And either way, you win, by keeping yourself active and interested in the world around you. The time of the rest of your life is in your hands.

RESOURCES

Books:

Most of the books listed at the end of Chapter 3, on retirement, are good sources on planning for and living the retired life. Additional sources that focus on how to live the life are listed below.

Burgett, G. (1999). *How to Create Your Own Super Second Life; What Are You Going to Do With Your Extra 30 Years?* Santa Maria, CA: Communications Unlimited. A list of 200 planning activities as well as planning tools are designed to help you organize and enjoy a full life in your 60s and beyond.

Cantor, D. and Thompson, A. (2001). *What Do You Want to Do When You Grow Up?: Starting the Next Chapter of Your Life.* New York: Little Brown & Company. Cantor is a psychologist who offers a path to developing a fulfilling and satisfying life, including taking an inventory and making a plan based on the self-discovery process.

Fetridge, G. (1994). *The Adventure of Retirement.* Amherst, NY: Prometheus Books. This is a practical handbook covering all areas of life in retirement and offering a thorough list of appropriate activities and resources.

Heilman, J. (2002). *Unbelievably Good Deals & Great Adventures That You Absolutely Can't Get Unless You're Over 50.* New York: McGraw-Hill Books. This is a book for people looking for information on how to save money on all aspects of travel.

Smith, M. and Smith, S. (2000). *101 Secrets for a Great Retirement: Practical, Inspirational, & Fun Ideas for the Best Years of Your Life!* New York: McGraw-Hill. The Smiths, who also wrote *The Retirement Sourcebook* listed in Chapter 3, have written an informative and encouraging compendium of ways to a successful retirement.

Seligman, M. (2002). *Authentic Happiness.* New York: Simon & Schuster. Seligman offers the results of his research and practical ways to become more authentically and deeply happy.

Wagner, T. and Day, B. (2002). *How to Enjoy Your Retirement: Activities from A to Z (2nd edition).* VanderWyk & Burnham. This listing of interesting and enriching ideas for enjoying retirement includes telephone numbers, web sites and addresses.

Web Sites:

The first site gives further information from the book discussed in this chapter; the rest of the list is a sampling from the wide array of web sites for activities that may enrich your 60s and beyond.

The Authentic Happiness web site (www.authentichappiness.org) offers information on Dr. Seligman's theory and research and includes the instrument for identifying your signature strengths.

American Automobile Association (www.aaa.com) is a resource for travel information—maps, routes, reservations; roadside assistance; and driver improvement classes that cover defensive driving and updates on state laws.

AmeriCorps*VISTA (www.americorps.org) invites volunteers to work in nonprofits, public agencies and faith-based groups in the U.S. to fight illiteracy, improve health services, create businesses and increase housing opportunities.

The Chautauqua Institution (www.ciweb.org) is a non-profit educational center in New York State, founded in 1874, that offers week-end and week-long programs in arts, education, religion and recreation, including programs geared to the 55-Plus.

Earthwatch Institute (www.earthwatch.org) promotes sustainable conservation of natural resources and cultural heritage through research, education and conservation projects in partnership with scientists, the public, educators and business.

Elderhostel, Inc. (www.elderhostel.org) calls itself "the nation's first and the world's largest education and travel organization for adults 55 and over." They offer more than 10,000 programs around the world which include lodging, classes and excursions.

Executive Service Corps (www.escus.org) uses volunteers from business, the professions and nonprofit organizations to provide low-cost consultants for nonprofits who need help.

Habitat for Humanity International (www.habitat.org) works to eliminate poverty housing and homelessness around the world by inviting volunteers to help build houses in partnership with families who need them.

International Executive Service Corps (www.iesc.org) works to increase the competitiveness of small-and medium-size firms in the developing world, using volunteers who share their knowledge and skills to further this goal.

North Carolina Center for Creative Retirement (www.unca.edu/ncccr/) provides educational opportunities for people 50 and over; this site offers links to similar centers in a number of other states.

Outward Bound USA (www.outwardbound.com) offers "adventure-education" programs emphasizing personal growth through challenging wilderness experiences that are paced for the ability of participants.

Partners of the Americas (www.partners.net) is a volunteer-based organization with projects that promote social, economic, and cultural development through partnerships with Latin American and Caribbean countries.

Peace Corps (www.peacecorps.gov) accepts volunteers of all ages. They serve in 70 countries, carrying out a wide range of service activities and projects.

SeniorNet (www.seniornet.org) is a non-profit organization of computer-using adults age 50 and above, providing education, discussion groups, and discounts on computer-related and other products and services.

9

Choosing to Build Meaning into the Last Third of Your Life

We humans, unique among all living things, seek meaning. From the most ancient recorded times to the present we have sought to understand the reasons for our lives, to reach beyond ourselves to something transcending our limitations. One of the basic tasks facing us as part of each of the transitions during our adult lives is reconsidering our earlier choices about the answers to life's most basic questions. As Gail Sheehy emphasizes in *New Passages*, "The paramount concern of the sixties is: *What will my life add up to? Is it too late to put more meaning into my life before I'm old?*"

Well into middle age Arnie was best known as the town drunk—a disgrace to himself, a failure to his wife and an embarrassment to his six children. However, at the memorial when he died in his early 70s, dozens of people from his small mill town stood to attest to his having been the most important person in their lives. In fact, several swore they were alive only because of him. Some of his family and old friends, who mainly recalled the bad years, expressed amazement that the failure they knew had done so much for so many during his sixties.

Arnie suffered a terrible childhood. His mother died of cancer when he was seven, and his father was a child abuser—with Arnie as his main target. Although he was gifted intellectually, being a child of abuse and the great depression he felt lucky to finish high school and escape home. There was no college for him despite his brilliance.

All his adult life Arnie did things to extremes. He smoked too much, he ate too much, he gambled too much, and—worst of all—he drank too much. Despite all this, plus bouts of bad health, he was able to work steadily as his six children grew—a testament to his innate ability. Unfortunately, despite a good paying job, he provided poorly for his family because of his bad habits and his generosity to anyone needing help. That plus his alcoholism alienated several of his children and old friends. Some later forgave him while others never did. His first wife, the mother of his children, finally divorced him.

One day he realized that by himself he could not beat the demons that hounded him. Although not formally a religious person, he said he always felt there was some greater power that could help him if he reached for it. With this hope, he asked for help from Alcoholics Anonymous where at long last he found a meaningful outlet for his enormous talents. Once his own addiction was under control, he devoted the rest of his life to helping others in need—both alcoholics and people in the community who needed other kinds of help.

The testimonials at his memorial ranged from women who swore that Arnie's help was all that saved them from despair and death to neighbors who shared how he had led them in saving the neighborhood park. All agreed he would listen forever to anyone who asked for his help—even in the middle of the night—and that he always had positive ideas as to how problems could be solved and lives salvaged. On top of all that, he made the world's best fruitcake—one of which went each year to every one of the hundreds of people he knew and loved. During his fifties and sixties, Arnie, the town drunk, had found meaning in life which turned him into a local hero.

As has been historically the case for a majority of human kind, most Americans in the twenty-first century make choices about the meaning of their lives within some religious or spiritual framework. Typical for Americans, an enormous range of spiritual and religious traditions are open to us. Numerous studies have found answers to the following key questions which may help you build meaning into your life:

- Is there any scientific evidence supporting the need for meaning in order for you to live a full, satisfying life?

- Do happiness, good physical health, good mental health and long life correlate positively with religious and spiritual involvement?

- Do people tend to become more religious and spiritual as they grow older?

- Do most Americans 60 and above consider religious and spiritual issues important?

- Do certain practices usually connected to religious or spiritual commitments such as prayer and contemplation, in themselves, contribute to health and happiness?

While the meaning of religion can be ambiguous, most of us have a similar understanding of what "being religious" means. However, understanding what "being spiritual" means is more difficult. Therefore, before we look in more detail at the research findings, a working definition of "spiritual" is in order. As David Moberg, Ph.D., points out in *Aging and Spirituality*, dozens of definitions exist. Perhaps a couple of the more thoughtful of these will suffice here. According to Moberg, "The definition of spirituality that was used in the landmark Spiritual Well-Being Section of the 1971 White House Conference on Aging centered around people's inner resources, especially their 'ultimate concern, the basic value around which all other values are focused, the central philosophy of life—whether religious, antireligious, or nonreligious—which guides a person's conduct, the supernatural and nonmaterial dimensions of human nature.'"

In *The Holy Longing* Ronald Rolheiser posits a similar, but more dynamic definition:

> Hence, spirituality is not about serenely picking or rationally choosing certain spiritual activities like going to church, praying or meditating, reading spiritual books, or setting off on some explicit spiritual quest. It is far more basic than that. Long before we do anything explicitly religious at all, we have to do something about the fire that burns within us. What we do with that fire, how we channel it, is our spirituality. Thus, we all have a spirituality whether we want one or not, whether we are religious or not. Spirituality is more about whether or not we can sleep at night than about whether or not we go to church. It is about being integrated or falling apart, about being within community or being lonely, about being in harmony with Mother Earth or being alienated from her. Irrespective of whether or not we let ourselves be consciously shaped by any explicit religious idea, we act in ways that leave us either healthy or unhealthy, loving or bitter. What shapes our actions is our spirituality.

Thus, as you read on, it is important to understand the breadth of the term "spirituality" as we use it in this chapter. People can be spiritual without being religious and also can be involved in religious activities without being spiritual. In fact, as defined above, the term clearly includes people who might not define themselves as spiritual. While some of us do find our spirituality within a formal religious or spiritual tradition, many others of us find our meaning in life through commitments beyond themselves to things such as political causes, environmental preservation, family, or scientific study. That something beyond ourselves which gives meaning to our lives is what we mean by spiritual in this chapter.

Now that we have a sense of what spirituality means, let us look at how studies and experts answer the questions concerning the search for meaning, its relationship to spiritual and religious commitments and practices, their effect on health and happiness, and the choices you have that can help you live what Martin Seligman, the author of *Authentic Happiness*, calls the *full* life.

Is there any scientific evidence supporting the need for meaning in order for you to live a full, satisfying life? From time immemorial philosophers and theologians have taught that life is not worth living without commitment to something greater than yourself, to something transcendent, to something or someone giving meaning to your existence. Recently psychological research has begun to verify that belief. This is illustrated by the congruence on the importance of meaning in the works of Martin Seligman, whom you met in earlier chapters, and Viktor Frankl, the famed psychotherapist and founder of Logotherapy.

Viktor Frankl, a Viennese M.D. and Ph.D. in philosophy who died in 1997 at the age of 92, had begun to stress the centrality of meaning in human life even before spending several years in Auschwitz concentration camp during World War II. In 1946 shortly after the his release from Auschwitz, he shared those ideas in his great classic *Man's Search for Meaning*, which recently had its 73rd printing, has been translated into 25 languages, and has sold over nine million copies in English alone. This book and his thirty-two others—mostly concerning the importance of meaning in human life—continue to influence a broad spectrum of thinkers even today.

As Frankl states in *The Will to Meaning*, "Man lives by ideals and values. Human existence is not authentic unless it is lived in terms of self-transcendence." In *The Unheard Cry for Meaning*, he adds, "Only to the extent that someone is living out this self-transcendence of human existence, is he truly human or does he become his true self. He becomes so, not by concerning himself with his self's actualization, but by forgetting himself and giving himself, over-looking himself and focusing outward." Writing in *Viktor Frankl's Contribution to Spirituality and Aging*, Scott Peterson summarizes Frankl's message: "It is in living for something greater, something other, than we ourselves which gives meaning to life. One's existence is a movement from 'being' to 'being in' and 'being for' something other, and it is in this movement that meaning is discovered which brings life, hope, and strength."

Based upon his experience and research as a medical doctor and psychotherapist, Frankl discovered we can find meaning in three ways: first, through what we give through creative works such as in our vocation; second, through what we take through experiencing things such as art, nature, and love; and third, and most important, through the attitude or stand we take toward suffering, guilt and death. Although "Frankl finds that human beings are oriented toward meaning and seek meaning in all circumstances," according to Dr. Melvin Kimble, his friend and editor of *Viktor Frankl's Contribution to Spirituality and Aging*, he also emphasizes that "because meaning is contextual it varies from individual to individual and from day to day…Each must see the meaning in his/her own con-text." Central to all of this is Frankl's insistence that we have a choice in these matters, that we must be responsible always. He emphasized this in his final book, his autobiography: "In the last analysis, getting old is an aspect of the transitoriness of human exist-ence. But this transitoriness can be a strong motivation for our responsibility—our recognition of responsibility as basic to human existence."

Sadly, after emphasizing the importance of finding meaning in life, Frankl points out that "more people today have the means to live but no meaning to live for." Martin Seligman makes a similar remark in *Authentic Happiness*: "The belief that we can rely on shortcuts to happiness, joy, rapture, comfort, and ecstasy, rather than be entitled to these feelings by the exercise of personal strengths and virtues leads to legions of people who in the middle of great wealth are starving spiritually. Positive emotion alienated from the exercise of character leads to emptiness, to inauthenticity, to depression, and, as we age, to the gnawing realization that we are fidgeting until we die."

However, in agreement with Frankl, the research of Seligman and his colleagues has proven that we can choose not to "fidget" our lives away. As he says, "Positive Psychology takes seriously the bright hope that if you find yourself stuck in the parking lot of life with few and only ephemeral pleasures, with minimal gratifications, and without meaning, there is a road out. This road takes you through the countryside of pleasure and gratification, up into the high coun-try of strength and virtue, and finally to the peaks of lasting fulfill-ment: meaning and purpose."

As discussed in the previous chapter, Seligman's research has shown how you can increase your pleasures so as to live a more *pleasant* life and how by using your signature strengths to increase authentic gratifications you can lead the *good* life. However, in the end he goes beyond these by saying that to lead a fully authentically happy life, you must also lead the *meaningful* life by "using your signature strengths in the service of something larger than you are," and, "the larger the entity to which you can attach yourself, the more meaning in your life."

Obviously, the works of Frankl and Seligman, both of whom come out of the Jewish tradition, suggest that choosing a spiritual or religious focus for your life can be important. In fact, after pointing out that he is not himself religious, Seligman says, "Religions instill hope for the future and create meaning in life…. The relation of hope for the future and religious faith is probably the cornerstone of why faith so effectively fights despair and increases happiness." This hints at the answer to our next question.

Do happiness, good physical health, good mental health and long life correlate positively with religious and spiritual involvement? In short, yes! Researchers agree that, on the average, people with religious or spiritual commitments and practices live longer, are physically ill less often and recover more quickly when ill, have better mental health and come out of depression more easily when it does occur, and are generally happier with their lives. Less agreement exists about exactly what causes what.

Evidence for longer life for those with strong spiritual commitments ranges from Snowdon's intuitive belief based upon knowing the subjects in the Nun Study to factual demographic findings.

After noting that his data, as such, said nothing on this topic, Snowdon points out that he believes strongly that the deep spirituality of the nuns increased their longevity. He adds, "My sense is that profound faith, like a positive outlook, buffers the sorrows and tragedies that all of us experience." Snowdon's insight has been verified by demographic studies. For example, according to Moberg, a demographic study published in 1999 involving 20,000 American adults "estimates that religious involvement prolongs life by about seven years."

In *Aging Well* Vaillant verifies this by reporting that the "Duke Longitudinal Study of Aging followed 252 older men for 25 years or until death intervened. They found that religious involvement in men was *negatively associated* with mortality," that is, the more religious men lived longer. This all makes sense because, as we shall see next, good physical health also correlates positively with religious practice.

As reported in *Aging and Spirituality,* a study in 1995 by Koenig summarizing the published studies on the topic concluded that there is a positive relation between religious beliefs and health: "For example, various studies have revealed an inverse relationship between religious commitment and hypertension, and strongly committed persons have significantly lower blood pressure, fewer strokes, better health, and less pain from cancer and other illness or surgery than similar persons with low religious commitment." There is really little debate about this. As Vaillant says in regard to religion and health, "The good news…is that religion works."

Insofar as longevity and physical health are concerned, the question is not about whether deeply spiritual or religious people generally live longer, healthier lives, but about which aspect of their lives causes it. Is it because of their spirituality or religiousness itself? Or is it because religious people tend to abuse alcohol less, smoke less, eat better diets, divorce less, and handle stress and depression and loss better? Or is because of some genetic trait that leads healthier people to become more spiritual? Or is it some combination of these? At present there is no certain answer to this "chicken/egg" issue. However, it's worth remembering a warning by Linda George, quoted in *Aging and Spirituality*, "The importance of religion for society and individuals is not going to rise or fall on what it does for health. We need to avoid the mentality that it just exists as a tool in the medicine chest to make people healthier." Finding meaning in your life has value far beyond health issues.

The relationship between good mental health and spirituality is somewhat more complex. While most studies show less depression among religious people and quicker recovery from depression when it occurs, studies of anxiety are more mixed with about half showing less among religious people, a quarter showing more, and the rest showing no difference, according to Moberg's summary of the research.

Moberg also points out that studies of religion and mental health often lump together persons who "internalize their faith and live it out regardless of consequences" and those "who use religion only to obtain status, security, self justification, health or sociability." Because the results for the two groups tend to be opposite, lumping them together tends to "cancel each other out." When those whose faith is internalized are separated out, Moberg says, research shows "they have higher self-esteem, better personality functioning, less paranoia, lower rates of depression, and less anxiety than their opposite number." Faking religiousness does not seem to work in improving mental health any more than it would as a way to find meaning in your life.

Moberg also reports on another study by Harold Koenig published in 1994. Koenig reported that when individuals over 50 experience a deep, sincere conversion to a religious perspective it typically "increases well being, resolves depression, frees from alcohol abuse, decreases anxiety, decreases selfishness, expands the desire to help others, and implants a new sense of purpose and hope." In a way, this simply confirms what Frankl and Seligman found—taking responsibility for finding meaning in something or someone outside of yourself can improve your well-being and happiness at any age.

Seligman himself has said as much: "Religious Americans are clearly less likely to abuse drugs, commit crimes, divorce, and kill themselves.... survey data consistently show religious people as being somewhat happier and more satisfied with life than nonreligious people." In fact, when Seligman lists five things research shows you can change in your life to raise your level of happiness, the fifth item is "Get religion."

As we saw in the earlier chapters on health, as you age, your self-perception of your health has nearly as much effect on your ability to function as does your actual health. Here too, religious involvement seems to matter. For example, in *Living to 100* Perls and Silver note, "In a 1982 study of 1,459 persons aged 65 and over, religious attendance was more closely related to satisfaction with health than were gender, age, race, education, marital status, working status, alcohol use, smoking or recent hospitalization." After having earlier noted that religious commitment is positively related to subjective well-being, Moberg reemphasizes this in concluding his review of the research by stating, "This chapter summarizes the overwhelming evidence from research that high levels of religiousness and spirituality are correlated positively with life satisfaction, health, healing, and well-being."

Do people tend to become more religious and/or spiritual as they grow older? Do most Americans 60 and above consider religious and spiritual issues important? Research findings are all over the place as to the answer to the first question, but the answer to the second is clearly positive.

Concerning whether those 60 and above usually become more religious and/or spiritual, Stevens-Long and Commons in *Adult Life* summarize the research by stating bluntly that the common belief that elderly people become more religious is incorrect. At the other extreme, after also reviewing the research on the topic, Moberg concludes, "With few exceptions, research on numerous groups of Americans has shown that the levels of religious beliefs, behavior, and experiences that reflect spirituality increase with age." He even goes on to point out that the more recent studies prove that this finding is not a cohort effect, that is, it has continued to be true as different generations have aged. On the other hand, he recognizes that some of the increase may result simply from the fact that religiously committed people live longer.

In the middle on this question is Vaillant, who to his surprise did not find an increase in spirituality among the men and women as they aged in the Harvard longitudinal study. In fact, as was also found in the Duke longitudinal study of aging, there was little change from midlife. Despite this, Vaillant insists, "In theory, spirituality *should* deepen in old age for all of us…. Aging slows us down and provides us time and peace to smell the flowers. Aging simplifies our daily routine and facilitates the acceptance of things we cannot change." In the end he concludes, "But, alas, as with wisdom, the jury is still out as to whether religious faith and spirituality really deepen in old age." Perhaps this is a good place to leave that question—especially since it seems less important than whether those 60 and above typically find spiritual matters important in their real lives.

In 1994 a Gallup Poll showed that among those 65 and over 76 percent said religion was very important in their lives with 52 percent reporting that they attended religious services at least weekly. Those figures are only a bit higher than for the American population as a whole where "about one-third consider religion to be the most important factor in their lives and another one-third considers it to be an important influence," according to Moberg. Likewise, in *Living to 100* Perls and Silver point out that "being part of God's plan is a key part of centenarians' self-concept, allowing them to cope with the inevitability and proximity of death." They also note that studies have shown that "among persons 65 and older, 82 percent say their religious beliefs are a very important influence in their lives." These findings are congruent with others reported in *Adult Life* that show about "75 percent of all Americans believe in life after death." Clearly, spiritual and religious commitments and activities are key factors in providing meaning in the lives of most Americans of every age and probably somewhat more so for those 60 and beyond.

Although the research does not provide detailed data on those who find meaning outside formal religious or spiritual traditions, it is important to recall the insistence of Rolheiser, Frankl and Seligman that meaning can be chosen in many other ways. For example, in the Pacific Northwest, where we live, a lower percentage of people believe in and participate in formal religious activities, but a much higher percentage find real meaning through other commitments and connections, such as to nature, to environmental and conservation causes, and to scientific endeavors, i.e., to things greater than and beyond themselves.

Do certain practices usually connected to religious or spiritual commitments such as prayer and contemplation, in themselves, contribute to health and happiness? As Snowdon puts it in *Aging with Grace*, "Evidence is now starting to accumulate from other studies that prayer and contemplation have a positive influence on long-term health and may even speed the healing process." Similarly, Perls and Silver report: "Harvard Medical School mind-body expert Herbert Benson has shown that frequent prayer, a feature of most religions, can lower blood pressure and reduce pain in cancer patients." Every great spiritual tradition, whether theistic or not, emphasizes setting aside time daily for contemplation, for quiet, for prayer or its secular equivalent. Things recommended for centuries by many spiritual traditions, such as breathing slowly and deeply with your eyes closed while letting your mind go quiet for a few minutes, are now known to have positive effects on both physical and mental health. Retreating from your everyday activities for a few hours or days to relax, contemplate, meditate and refocus the meaning in your life is another practice followed in many spiritual traditions which has proven to benefit health and happiness. Yoga has also become a common and highly effective example of this. Whether or not you are committed to a religious or spiritual tradition, such practices can benefit you too.

How can you choose to make the last third of your life meaningful? Now that we know what the studies show about spirituality and religion for those over 60, let us focus on the choices implied in that knowledge. If you are fortunate enough to already have transcendent meaning in your life upon which your strengths and virtues are focused, perhaps all you need is to choose to recommit yourself.

On the other hand, if you are one of those for whom the transition from work to free time has left an emptiness or if you are a person who has never found authentic happiness, there are a number of choices you can make in your 60s to change that. Based on his broad definition of spirituality which we saw at the start of this chapter, Rolheiser bluntly points out the consequence of failing to build transcendent meaning into your life, "The opposite of being spiritual is to have no energy, is to have lost all the zest for living—lying on a couch, watching football or sit-coms, taking beer intravenously!" Terrifying as such a fate may seem, it's the route chosen by default by many.

A vast range of ways exists in which you can build meaning into your life. For some, the very breadth of choice may present an obstacle. Nonetheless, as Seligman says, "Building strengths and virtues and using them in daily life are very much a matter of making choices." While taking responsibility, making commitments, and focusing outward are needed by all, the specifics of what you choose must fit your unique person and circumstances, as Frankl emphasized. No one can do this for you, but numerous support systems exist to aid you once you decide to make your life more meaningful.

The authors have each chosen a somewhat different route to building meaning into their lives. As a young adult John made a commitment to Christianity as postulated by the Catholic faith. At 70 this remains the central source of meaning in his life, and the church is the organizational framework in which he spent most of his work-life and is spending much of his volunteer time since retirement.

Delight has been committed to working with underprivileged adults, especially through her efforts with adult literacy. This has given meaning to her life beyond herself. But coming from an agnostic family, she has no strong ties to any church. At this time in her life, she wonders what she has missed, and how she might become more involved in spiritual growth.

If a label for Julie is required, she uses "humanist," perhaps preceded by "skeptical." She does not find a very active spiritual dimension in herself, though she respects the ethical principles that the great religions have in common. Her closest encounter with spirituality is in the outdoors: she never stops being awed at her first glimpse of Mount Rainier or the Olympic Mountains on a clear day, or the view into the Cascades from the top of the Mission Ridge ski run. Her gratification comes from time with her family and from volunteering, although she is still looking for the one great cause.

Every spiritual or religious group—whether theistic or nontheistic—has both people and proven practices ready and available to help. Tens of thousands of books, tapes, web sites, and pamphlets exist in hundreds of spiritual traditions open to anyone interested in investigating options. They can be of great assistance in helping you focus "the fire that burns within you." See the chapter resources for some good starting points.

After one warning, we will conclude with two examples of what finding meaning might entail. One example is from the secular, scientific tradition and the other from a liberal Christian tradition.

The warning: *You cannot fake meaning into your life! You must freely and truly choose it.*

The first example of an approach to finding meaning provides a way to avoid faking. It is the plan discussed earlier that Martin Seligman lays out for living the "full life." At its core his plan calls for taking the time to identify your own signature strengths, then focusing those strengths on the universal virtues he and his colleagues have identified as meaningful to all peoples throughout history: "wisdom and knowledge, courage, love and humanity, justice, temperance, and spirituality and transcendence." Finally, in Seligman's words, to have a totally meaningful life you must use your emotional strengths to "reach outside and beyond you to connect you to something larger and more permanent; to other people, to the future, to evolution, to the divine, or to the universe."

Our second example has evolved from a different tradition—a liberal Catholic one. In *The Holy Longing*, subtitled *The Search for a Christian Spirituality*, Ronald Rolheiser spells out what at first glance appears to be quite a different approach, but which, in fact, has much in common with Seligman's. Rolheiser summarizes by saying, "Generally, the following practices [form] the core of a healthy Christian spirituality: Regular prayer (both private and communal), the practice of charity and self-sacrifice (both at home and in the wider world), some concrete involvement with the poor, involvement within some church community, and a willingness to be vulnerable for love (as Christ was vulnerable)."

As stated earlier, these are but two examples from a vast array of opportunities to build more meaning into your life during your 60s. To answer Sheehy's question posited at the beginning of this chapter—*No, it is not too late in your 60s to put more meaning into your life. It is never too late to choose meaning!*

RESOURCES

Many of the books and web site resources listed in earlier chapters have relevance here including those in the chapters on mental health, relationships and especially those in the chapter on using your free time, where almost all the resources can be useful for anyone seeking specific outlets in which to develop meaning.

Because finding meaning in your life is such an integrated topic, there are no sub-categories in the resources below. Also, given the vastness of the literature in this area, no attempt is made to be comprehensive. For example, at this writing, in Amazon.com there are 32,000 books listed under "religion" and 19,000 under "spirituality." And web sites relating to religion, spirituality and meaning are beyond count. The following are, therefore, but a few samples of the range of works and web sites available.

Books:

Obviously, the great texts of world religions, such as the Bible or the Koran, are relevant here even though they are not listed below.

Autry, J. (2002). *The Spirit of Retirement: Creating a Life of Meaning and Personal Growth.* Roseville, CA: Prima Publishing. Using stories of successful retirees Autry demonstrates the importance of meaningfully using your free time after retirement. The book has been described as both pragmatic and spiritual.

Berg. Y. (2002). *The Power of Kabbalah: This Book Contains the Secrets of the Universe and the Meaning of Our Lives.* San Diego, CA: Jodere Group. Rabbi Berg's work provides one Jewish perspective on how to find meaning in life. It's inexpensive and easy to read.

Fischer, K. (1998). *Winter Grace: Spirituality and Aging.* Nashville, TN: Upper Room. Although this is written from a Christian tradition, it's a superb work for anyone searching for meaning in the latter years of life.

Karren, K. (ed.). (2001). *Mind/Body Health: the Effects of Attitudes, Emotions, and Relationships (2nd edition).* San Francisco: Benjamin/Cummings. This book previously listed in the relationships chapter also contains a long section on "Spirituality and Health" as part of its presentation of findings on how the mind affects health.

Kimble, M. (ed.) (2000). *Victor Frankl's Contribution to Spirituality and Aging.* Binghamton, NY: The Hawthorn Pastoral Press. This anthology summarizes those aspects of Frankl's writing that deal specifically with spirituality, which he defined very broadly.

Koenig, H. (1994). *Aging and God: Spiritual Pathways to Mental Health in Midlife and Later Years.* Binghamton N.Y.: Hawthorn Press. Koenig, an M.D. and Director of the Duke University Center for the Study of Religion/Spirituality and Health, reviews scientific findings showing that successful aging is facilitated by religious and spiritual beliefs and behaviors.

Leonard, G. & Murphy, M. (1995). *The Life We Are Given: A Long-Term Program for Realizing the Potential of Body, Mind, Heart, and Soul.* N.Y.: J.P. Tarcher. Written by men, famed for leading others on spiritual quests, who have now experienced their sixties, this book offers a long-term plan for human growth—a spiritual but not religious approach.

Moberg, D. (ed.) (2001). *Aging and Spirituality: Spiritual Dimensions of Aging Theory, Research, Practice, and Policy.* Binghamton, NY: The Hawthorn Press. As mentioned in the chapter, this book, written from a protestant, Christian perspective, offers an in-depth look at the research on how aging, religion and spirituality intersect.

Nasr, S. (ed.) (1991). *Islamic Spirituality II: Manifestations (World Spirituality, Vol 20).* N.Y.: Crossroads/Herder & Herder. One of a series, this anthology reviews various aspects of spirituality from an Islamic perspective.

Rolheiser, R. (1999) *The Holy Longing: The Search for a Christian Spirituality.* N.Y.: Doubleday. For those seeking a Catholic perspective on spirituality, there is no better book than this. It's easy to read, practical and profound.

Rosenberg, L. (2001). *Living in the Light of Death: On the Art of Being Truly Alive.* Boston: Shambhala Publications. Looking at the meaning of life and death from a Buddhist perspective, Rosenberg emphasizes that life can and should be lived joyfully despite death's inevitability.

Seligman, M. (2002). *Authentic Happiness.* N.Y.: The Free Press. As discussed in the chapter, this book can help anyone live a meaningful life.

Walsh, R. (2000). *Essential Spirituality: The 7 Central Practices to Awaken Heart and Mind.* Hoboken, NJ: John Wiley & Sons. Drawing on the world's major religions, Walsh, a psychiatrist and philosopher, identifies seven practices that can help you improve your life and world. He both explains the practices and presents practical exercises for integrating them into your life.

Web Sites:

As with books, a vast number of web sites might be listed under this topic, e.g., nearly every church, synagogue, and mosque has its own web site, as do all significant non-religious groups promoting spirituality in its broadest sense. Therefore, what follows is a mere sampling of the range of sites possible, with emphasis on several that have links to other relevant sites plus those oriented toward aging.

The Center for Aging, Religion & Spirituality (www.aging-religion-spirituality.com) provides excellent links on this topic as well as information from a Lutheran perspective.

The Center for Gerontology, Spirituality, and Faith (www.spirituality4aging.org) has excellent information and links specifically relating to seniors and spiritual life. This center is based in Christianity, but is open to a broad perspective.

The Center for Mindfulness in Medicine, Health Care, and Society at the University of Massachusetts (www.umassmed.edu/cfm/history.cfm) is an outgrowth of the Stress Reduction Clinic, founded by Jon Kabat-Zinn. It is a good example of how practices developed over centuries by various religious and spiritual groups can be useful in themselves. As their web site says, "'Mindfulness-Based Stress Reduction' goes far beyond what is commonly thought of as 'stress reduction' and may be best described as tapping directly into the dimensions of human experience commonly described with words such as *heart, spirit, soul, Tao,* and *dharma.* In this way, MBSR can be thought of as a consciousness discipline: a profound spiritual discipline, aimed at deep self-reflection, self-knowledge, and liberation from confining views of self, others, and the world."

The Center for the Study of Religion/Spirituality and Health (www.dukespiritualityandhealth.org/index.html) as well as its affiliated Duke University Center for the Study of Aging and Human Development (www.geri.duke.edu/index.html) provide resources and excellent links regarding scientific studies and resources on this and other topics relating to aging.

The web site of the Forum on Religion, Spirituality and Aging (FORSA) (www.asaging.org/forsa.html) says it "constitutes a national, multidisciplinary and nondenominational community of professionals committed to examining and fostering the spiritual dimension of human existence as a central element in the aging process and to fostering an appreciation for the importance of incorporating an awareness of this dimension into all the disciplines that make up the fascinating world of gerontology. Some members come at the topic from traditional faith perspectives and are active in various churches, synagogues and mosques, while others approach the issues from the perspective of 'mindful' or 'conscious' aging. Whatever your particular perspective, you are welcome to become part of the dialogue of a most worthwhile and welcoming professional society. FORSA is a constituent group of the American Society on Aging (ASA), the largest professional membership association in the field of aging" (www.asaging.org/). The forum publishes the journal *Aging & Spirituality*.

10

It's Your Choice!

You've heard it, and it's true: Getting old ain't for sissies. But let's be honest—neither is adolescence, with its acne and angst. The mating game isn't exactly a piece of cake either. And once you've found a relationship, the struggle to make it work, or the pain of breaking up—that's easy? How about your work life, whether you manage a home or a business—hasn't that brought you some tension, frustration, disappointment? So what's new about life after 60? As this book has been saying, what's new is some of the choices you have to make, and the pleasure, if you accept it, of recognizing how many choices you have at this stage of your life.

Using our own life experiences and those of people we know personally or have learned about through investigating the subject, we have become convinced of a few key factors leading to a satisfying life after 60. Perhaps the essential message about all of them is that you need to *pay attention.* Because in a way it's your last chance, you must not take for granted these basic factors of a good life:

- your relationships with family and friends;

- your health, the entwined elements of mental and physical health;

- the decisions you make about retiring and about all the business aspects of life;

- the ways you use this most precious time; and

- your connection to the transcendent, to spirituality and religion.

We hope this book has stimulated you to think in a more focused way about some of these matters, to join us in looking attentively at the use we are making of whatever gifts of time, health and prosperity we have. We hope that the lists of resources have lured you into doing some research of your own on the issues that are most interesting or pressing for you, and that from that process you have gained new insight or direction that enlightens the choices you make.

For one last reminder of what we've learned, here is a list of our top thirty choices.

<u>Your Top Thirty Choices</u>:

<u>OK or</u>
<u>Needs work</u>:

1. Develop and maintain positive relations with family and friends. _____

2. Have at least one intimate, confidential relationship. _____

3. Never let yourself become isolated from others. _____

4. Maintain as healthy a sex life as your situation permits. _____

5. Commit time and energy to "something larger than you are." _____

6. Give to others through activities that interest and excite you. _____

7. Use spiritual practices, such as meditation or prayer, in daily living. _____

8. Identify your signature strengths and use them often. _____

9. Think long and hard about whether to retire. _____

10. Enjoy life, e.g., get involved in the arts as producer or consumer. _____

11. Laugh a lot. _____

12. If you smoke, quit! If you can't, get help! Then quit. _____

13. Do not abuse alcohol. If you do, get help! _____

14. Keep your weight near normal. If you can't, get help. _____

15. Eat a balanced diet. Eat with a friend at least once a day. _____

16. Do both strength and aerobic exercise—use it or lose it. _____

17. Floss and have your teeth cleaned. _____

18. Get the recommended flu and pneumonia shots. _____

19. Know and act upon the symptoms of serious disease. _____

20. Use your mind a lot—read, study, do puzzles—use it or lose it. _____

21. Develop an optimistic outlook on life. _____

22. If you get depressed, get help. It's curable. _____

23. Enjoy the past, plan wisely for the future, but focus on now. _____

24. Plan ahead to assure financial independence. _____

25. Know your assets, Social Security and other retirement benefits. _____

26. Create or update your will, your "living will" and directives. _____

27. Investigate and decide upon long term care insurance. _____

28. Tell those close to you about your end-of-life decisions. _____

29. Give up old animosities. _____

30. Pay attention—choices count! _____

Finally, the choices are yours. What is best for you may not be the same for another person. What matters is that you know yourself, your strengths, your loves, your enthusiasm, and your opportunities. Then make the most of them by making wise choices.

Life after 60? You bet! There's a whole lot of life after 60. Choose wisely and enjoy it all.

978-0-595-37538-7
0-595-37538-3

Made in the USA
Lexington, KY
19 December 2010